A Year in the Guard
Company A
1st Eastern Shore Maryland Infantry, U.S.

by Kimberly B. Baynard

ISBN 978-1-105-77676-2

Manufactured by lulu.com

Dedicated to the memory of Private Levin Adkins, Company A, 1st Eastern Shore Md. Volunteers, whose family's story about the 'cavalry fort' initiated this project, and to the men of Company A who honorably served the United States to preserve the Union.

Thanks to my family, friends and co-workers who suggested resources and patiently listened to my project updates.

To Cayt and Ed: your advice and assistance with proofreading has been greatly appreciated.

And to Charles: Thanks for listening to my endless rambles, acting as my sounding board and accompanying me on visits to "Company A" sites. Our encounter with bureaucracy at the National Archives was particularly memorable! Thanks for all your support.

TABLE OF CONTENTS

Introduction p. 7

Chapter One: Maryland's Loyalties p. 9

Chapter Two: The Enlistment p.17

Chapter Three: Duty and Service p.31

Chapter Four: Company A p45

Chapter Five: Early Discharge p.57

Appendix-A: Shelltown Squad p.74

Appendix-B: Roll Call p.77

Cover Illustration: photograph of the Wallace Building, on the corner of Spring and Gay Streets in Cambridge, Maryland - site of the organization of the 1st Eastern Shore Maryland Volunteers.

Photograph by Kimberly B. Baynard

A Year in the Guard

Company A 1st Eastern Shore Maryland Infantry, U.S.

An Introduction

"The Summer of 1860, being the time for the nominations of candidates for the presidential chair of the United States of America, nominations were made by the several parties existing at that time. The Democrat Party met at Charleston, S.C., and there being a division in the party they split and part of them met in Baltimore City. Wool–dyed Democrats nominated John C. Breckenridge of Kentucky and Lane of Arkansas, and the Free Soil Democrats that met in Baltimore, nominated Stephen A. Douglas of Illinois and Hershell V. Johnson of Georgia. The Union or People Party met in convention in Baltimore City and nominated John Bell of Tennessee and Edward Everett of Massachusetts. The Republicans of the country met in convention at Chicago and nominated Abraham Lincoln of Illinois and Hamlin of Maine.....

"The Democratic Party was defeated. Lincoln and Hamlin, the Republican nominees, were elected President and Vice President of these United States. This so enraged the people of the South that they would not submit to the rule of Lincoln and Hamlin. They began to oppose the constituted authorities of the government and passed laws in defiance of the laws of the United States. South Carolina passed a secession ordinance, declaring herself out of the Union. Other states followed soon after.

"The President-elect could not take his seat until the fourth of March 1861, and James Buchanan, the President sat on his seat and let the South take the government forts and arsenals and the public property in the South without trying to do anything to prevent them.

He said he had not the power to coerce them and refused to reinforce Fort Sumter in Charleston Harbor.

"The President-elect, Abraham Lincoln, took his seat on the fourth day of March 1861, and began his rule under trying times. The whole country was in confusion and tumult at Fort Sumter. The first gun was fired April 12, 1861; there was no communication between the fort and government. The Charleston people had built Batteries all around the fort. At this time, the government sent reinforcements for Fort Sumter but they could not get to the fort. Major Anderson who had command, surrendered April 14 after two days of bombardment. They saluted the flag and marched out with all the honors of war. No one was hurt in the attack on the fort. Then the President called out 75,000 volunteers for three months. The first battle was fought at Bull Run about 25 miles from Washington in the State of Virginia; this was in July 1861. The Union forces were defeated. They were commanded by Gen. McDowell and the rebel forces were commanded by Gen. Beauregard.

"After that the President called for 300,000 volunteers, and I myself, having nothing to do, concluded to enlist. James Wallace, a lawyer of our town, got authority from the government to raise a regiment for service on the Eastern Shore of Maryland. John C. Henry, a young man of our town, received authority from Col. Wallace to raise a company for this regiment and I enlisted in this company, which was designated afterward as Company A, the first Company. I enlisted on Sept. 11, 1861; and the recruits for the company encamped out on the road near Jacktown......." [i]

Pvt. Levin W. Bothum

Co. A, 1st Eastern Shore Volunteers, U.S.

Chapter One

Maryland's Loyalties

The State of Maryland was of conflicted loyalties from the beginning of the American Civil War. Maryland, especially the Eastern Shore of Maryland, had much in common with the State of Virginia, who seceded from the Union on April 17, 1861. Southern and Eastern Maryland communities predominately consisted of citizens native to Maryland, descended, for the most part, from old colonial families. These communities were still largely dependent on an agricultural economy. Many Maryland slave-holders had begun freeing their slaves and by 1860 nearly half of the African American population in Maryland had been freed. [ii] However, many of the leading families still relied on slave labor. The Western Shore of Maryland was becoming industrial, less dependent on the agricultural economy found on the Eastern Shore, and had more in common with the northern states. Northern communities had a growing immigrant population, thriving commercial economy and fewer slave-holders.

Maryland's loyalties were put to the test on April 19, 1861 when Union troops were called to Washington to defend the Capital in the event of an attack by the Confederate Army. Train loads of soldiers arrived in Baltimore from the north. At that time, trains did not pass through the city therefore making it necessary to transfer from one train line to another to continue one's journey. The Federal soldiers headed for Washington disembarked at President Street Station and marched along Pratt Street to Camden Station where they were to embark for Washington on another train. A large number of citizens in sympathy with the South were outraged that Union troops were in their city and they gathered in protest. A riot ensued, with Baltimoreans attacking Union soldiers with stones and bricks. The fleeing soldiers were forced to defend themselves and fired into the crowd. Four soldiers and twelve civilians were killed and many more were wounded. [iii]

With more troops on their way, General Benjamin Butler bypassed the Baltimore railroad altogether. He transported his troops by boat and landed in Annapolis, Maryland. To further ensure the safe passage of troops through Maryland, General Butler stationed troops on Federal Hill overlooking Baltimore.

Maryland's decision of whether or not to secede was of great interest in Washington. The nation's capital was located between Virginia and Maryland. If Maryland were to follow Virginia's example, Washington would be surrounded by Confederate states and likely be lost to The South. Leaders in Washington kept a careful watch on Maryland leaders. After much delay, the Maryland State Legislature met in Frederick to vote on whether Maryland should secede from the Union. Approximately thirty delegates of known secessionist sympathies were arrested to prevent their attendance. The legislature voted against secession. [iv] Though many Marylanders enlisted and fought on both sides of the conflict, the State would remain under Federal control for the duration of the War, ensuring her 'neutral' status.

Though the Eastern Shore is usually considered to have been predominately loyal to The South, many individuals and communities remained loyal to the preservation of The Union. During a state-wide vote to consider whether a convention to discuss the possibility of Maryland's secession should be held, Talbot County voted in support of The Union. The towns of St. Michaels and Trappe were particularly supportive. Cambridge of

Dorchester County and Chestertown of Kent County each raised a regiment of troops for the U. S. Army.

It should be noted that even among Union supporters, there were conflicting opinions. Pro-Union sympathies did not necessarily indicate an opposition to slavery. Though there were certainly those who were against the continuation of slavery, many supported the North because of their intense devotion to The Union that their fore-fathers had fought so hard to establish.

"A sure thing – that nine tenths of the Union men now in arms will lay them down whenever they come to believe that the war is waged to liberate the negroes."

from the Regimental Flag, the camp newspaper of the 2nd Delaware Infantry while stationed in Eastern Virginia.

Lieutenant Adjutant John E. Rastall from Milwaukee, Wisconsin joined abolitionists in Kansas before the war, raiding slave-holding villages. He was arrested and escaped back to Wisconsin. At the start of the war, Rastall enlisted as Private in the 5th Wisconsin Infantry, Company B. He was soon discharged so that he could accept a position with the 1st Eastern Shore Md Volunteers organized in Cambridge, Md. In a letter home from Salisbury he writes:

".... must stop sending me the Sentinel (local Wisconsin newspaper). *It is altogether too rabid for this section, which I cannot disguise. Almost all our officers are slave holders ..... apt to get into trouble in consequence of its editorials. The last sheet contained an article advocating the freeing of all slaves, wherever the U.S. Army should go. That thing won't ... and any man who advocates that doctrine is a fool. If I thought for a minute that the object of our government was the emancipation of the slaves*

after ... "Lovejoy" style I should resign certain. You may send me a "News" but don't send any more Sentinels....."

v February1862

Even among family, loyalties were divided. As throughout the country, families were torn when members chose opposing sides in the conflict. John C. Henry, Captain of Company A, 1st Eastern Shore Maryland Volunteers and later Private in Company A, 2nd Maryland C.S. was living with his parents in Cambridge and employed as a clerk when the war broke out. In a letter to his mother Wilhelmina Goldsborough Henry he writes :

"Camp – near Hanover Junction.

February 21, 1864

My dearest Friend:

Seated quietly in my hut, I find my thoughts wandering (as they always do in my leisure moments) to my home. I have remembered that this evening is the anniversary of my departure from all those who I love and hold dear. Let us look back together – (for I believe that our thoughts this evening are the same.) We will begin this evening one year ago; everything being prepared for my journey, I started for the Confederacy, but before leaving, let us look at the picture at my loved home: Reclining on the sofa in the old front sitting room (you well know the hour) is my Father; my sister Lizzie is sitting by his side. In my Grand-mother's room sat that dear old lady, Mr. B, and my little sister Willie, who, upon my entering the room, threw a gaze full upon me as she never had done before, (but perhaps it was my conscience that gave it this appearance) for I felt that I should have let you know my intentions, but I could not – I feared to venture. The time spent there was but a few minutes, for my time was growing short. In the dining room sat my Mother! My Mother! Kneeling by her side was my little brother Hampton, saying his prayers. (I felt that his prayers were being sent up to Heaven in my behalf.) I took a farewell look at my Mother, and left my home – only for a while! I hope to return and find all those, whom I dearly love, living in peace and happiness in the fear of their Maker. I reached Richmond early in March; joined the Army and have passed safely through the battles of Winchester and Gettysburg, protected only by my God, and why should I fear the coming contest; the same kind Providence, Who watched over me then, will continue His watch; then why should you, my friend, grieve at our separation?

The October campaign will soon be upon us. It is probable that our Battalion will remain inactive, stationed where we now are, but should we not, there will of course be casualties among us. I, therefore have one request to ask of you – don't believe any reports. There are several men of the same name as myself in the Battalion, and if anything should happen to me, I have good and kind friends who will take care of me and inform you, or some of my family.

I received, per Truce, letters from my Mother and sister Willie, of date January 24th and 30th. I was very sorry to hear of the death of two of our friends. Many have been their messages during my absence. Remember me kindly to the family of the latter and assure them that I sympathize with them deeply in their distress. Though we differ in our sentiments, I can never forget their kindness, and I do not allow any prejudices to enter my bosom that will cause me to cast off those who have been tried and proven to be truest of friends....give my love to everybody,

Your affectionate friend, *"C"* [vi]

Across the above letter was written:

"Sunday, February 28th

I thought this was far on its way, for I sent it off nearly a week ago, but it proves to have been lost, and the finder, knowing the hand-writing, has returned it to me. I have a friend who leaves for Baltimore tomorrow. He will take this for me. I received a Flag of Truce letter from my Mother day before yesterday, dated February 7th. Was glad to hear that all are well. Clem did not come up as I expected. Tho he will come up in a few days. Please hand the enclosed to cousin Winder.....

I hope Cousin J's business will be well established by the time the war ends, and have no doubt it will, for there is no prospect of peace. We are in a better condition than ever before, and nearly all the troops are re-enlisting for 40 years or the war, showing that we never intend to yield, but all will be well.

Goodbye. -Yours affectionately, "C"

Following is a letter to J. C. Henry from his mother at home in Cambridge, Md.:

"*Cambridge, Oct. 7th*

Every week I write to you, my darling boy, via Fortress Monroe, and hope my letters have reached you; have been longing for a reply, and will still hope on. Johnie, darling, always think of us as full of devoted love for you. Your leaving home without our knowledge, and entertaining different views from what we think right, has made me sometimes fear you may suppose our love for you has lessened, but that can never be. Our hearts are filled with sorrow, not anger, and our affection, if possible, greater, because you are separated from us. My faith is strong that a kind Father will answer my never ceasing prayers and preserve you in health and safety. Think of us, my darling, as having you ever in our thoughts. All of us are well.....

Your devoted Mother,

Willie Henry."

John C. Henry returned to Cambridge after the War and married Ann E. Lake in 1866, with whom he had several children. He worked as a clerk in Cambridge and later moved to New Orleans, Louisiana.

Chapter Two
The Enlistment

"Col. James Wallace, Cambridge, Md.:

Sir, - The regiment of infantry you offer is accepted for three years, or during the war, provided you have it ready for marching orders in sixty days. In accordance with the letter of Governor Hicks of the 15th inst., you will be mustered into the service of the United States to act as a home guard, to be stationed on the Eastern Shore of Maryland.

By Order of the Secretary of War,

James Lesley, Jr., Chief Clerk." [vii]

James Wallace (1818 – 1887) was a native of Dorchester County, Maryland and practiced law in the town of Cambridge. The Wallace family lived on Gay St. at the site of the current Dorchester County Library. They also had a farm east of town near Jacktown, probably in the vicinity of today's Hyatt Regency Resort. At the start of the Civil War, Wallace was authorized by the United States Army to organize a regiment for the security of the Eastern Shore. Recruitment began in September 1861 at his law office on the corner of Gay and Spring Streets. His regiment was called the 1st Eastern Shore Volunteers, or the Home Guard, and consisted of ten companies of infantry.

1st EASTERN SHORE HOME GUARD

Company	Location organized
Co. A	Cambridge, Dorchester County
Co. B	Strait's District, Dorchester County
Co. C	Church Creek, Dorchester County
Co. D	Greensboro, Caroline County
Co. E	Preston, Caroline County
Co. F	Denton, Caroline County
Co. G	Federalsburg, Caroline County
Co. H	Trappe, Talbot County
Co. I	Baltimore City
Co. K	Annamessex, Somerset County

Colonel Wallace advertised for volunteers for the 1st Eastern Shore Home Guard in the Cambridge Herald and Easton Gazette. His advertisements assured potential recruits that they would be stationed on the Eastern Shore and outlined the pay levels and other details about the organization of the regiment.

The Cambridge Herald

MARYLANDERS, RALLY!!
VOLUNTEERS WANTED
FOR THE
1ST EASTERN SHORE REGIMENT
OF
HOME GUARD.

I HAVE been authorized by the War Department at Washington to have enrolled and mustered into the service of the United States a Regiment of Infantry to act as a

HOME GUARD,

AND TO BE STATIONED ON THE

Eastern Shore of Maryland.

The purpose of the movement is to repel invasion, to preserve the peace and good order in our midst and to protect the rights of all, and aid in the enforcement of the laws.

As it has been asserted, with a view of defeating the movement, that the administration intend ordering the troops away from home as soon as they are mustered in. I would remark that the Secretary of War expressly pledges that they "shall be stationed on the Eastern Shore of Maryland" and used only for "Home Protection". I state this fact for the benefit of those who are willing to do all they can for their country in its present peril, but whose circumstances are such as prevents their going abroad. The necessity of this movement must be apparent to every candid and considerate mind. We are already threatened by the enemies of the country. – At any moment we are liable to have civil war in our midst. In times of Revolution no one can tell into what peril a single day may place us. It behooves us to prepare, and be ready for any emergency, ere it be too late. - It is high time that Marylanders were

armed and prepared to protect themselves against adventuring Rebels.

The TIME OF ENLISTMENT will be three years, or until the end of the War.

A COMPANY consists, when full, of One Captain, Two Lieutenants, One First Sergeant, Four Sergeants, Eight Corporals, Two Musicians, One Waggoner, and Eighty-two Privates.

Each Company will select its own officers, subject to the approval of the War Department.

The Company will be mustered into service as soon as it numbers Eighty-six men. But must afterward be raised to One Hundred.

THE PAY allowed for a Captain is Sixty dollars, four rations per month and one servant,
Of First Lieutenant is Fifty dollars, four rations per month and one servant, Of Second Lieutenant is Forty-five dollars, four rations per month and one servant, Cadet, Twenty-four dollars per month, First Sergeant, Twenty dollars per month, Sergeant, Seventeen dollars per month, Corporal, Fifteen dollars per month, And Privates, Thirteen dollars per month. Those officers who have no rations mentioned above in their pay, are allowed one ration or nine dollars per month for food and three dollars per month for clothing. The same allowances are also made to Privates. Each soldier is entitled to a bounty of One Hundred Dollars when discharged from service.

THE DISPOSITION OF THE TROOPS.

As many inquiries have been made concerning the disposition of the companies, I would remark that the Government pays each man for his full time, and assumes that he will give the whole of his time to the service. But it is the evident and written intention of the Government to afford security to the homes of us all. To accomplish this it would appear to be necessary to keep each company stationed in the neighborhood in which it was organized, as

much as possible. Each company must be on muster every day. It is designated, I presume to let each company protect its own homes and neighborhood.

Such is the outline of the plan and its object. It will be modified as events and welfare of our people may demand. The details of the movement will be left to the commanding officer of the forces upon the Shore. For further particulars address,

JAMES WALLACE,

Col. 1st Eastern Shore Regiment of Home Guard,
Cambridge, Md.

Aug. 18, 1861

Early enlistees camped east of Cambridge on Colonel Wallace's farm near Jacktown. Shortly thereafter enough men had enlisted to warrant a trip into Caroline County for further recruitment. The newly recruited soldiers accompanied Colonel Wallace on a steamboat up the Choptank River to Potter's Landing south of Denton where they found Arthur Willis also in the process of enlisting a regiment for the Eastern Shore. [viii] Mr. Willis had been authorized by Major General John A. Dix and was assisted by Lieutenant Adjutant John E. Rastall recently of Co. B 5th Wisconsin Volunteer Infantry. Rastall had arrived from Baltimore on the steamer Kent to assist Mr. Willis and had set up camp in the vicinity of Potter's Landing. Upon the arrival of Colonel Wallace, the conflict of who was in charge became apparent. The issue was settled with Wallace relieving Willis of command. Lieutenant Adjutant Rastall transferred all supplies over to Colonel Wallace and accompanied the men back to Cambridge. Rastall was to act as Assistant to Wallace for the duration of the War. [ix]

According to one enlistee, Levin Bothum of Cambridge, officers were elected on the steamboat on their way back to town. Upon returning to Long Wharf at Cambridge, the men camped a few days at the Town Hall and were sworn into service in mid-September. [x] Men from Dorchester and neighboring counties arrived in Cambridge to enlist, and company leaders visited various towns in the area to recruit members. Company A was soon joined by not only additional companies from other areas of Dorchester and neighboring counties, but by troops from Delaware as well, accompanied by Brigadier General Henry H. Lockwood [xi], who was to command the numerous regiments.

The influx of military personnel must have caused quite a wave of excitement in the small town of Cambridge. At the beginning of the War, the town of Cambridge was bordered by the Choptank River to the north, Cambridge Creek to the east and Washington St. to the south. The main street heading west was Glasgow, leading toward the area around Hambrooks Bay. The town extended west roughly as far as Willis Street. The land east of the creek was a farm and wooded area accessed by what is now Dorchester Ave. The current bridge over Cambridge Creek did not exist until the development of East Cambridge and the coming of the railroad after the War. There was, however, a bridge over the creek in 1860 located a block or two from Main Street.[xii] It may have been at the end of Muir or Church Streets, where the creek narrows.

Cambridge was the county seat and relied on the large rural area of lower Dorchester County to support its numerous businesses. The 1860 Census for Cambridge lists a wide variety of occupations, as seen in the chart following:

OCCUPATIONS IN CAMBRIDGE IN 1860

Baker 2	Dentist 1	Miller 2	Shoe Maker 23	Clerk of Court 1
Barber 1	Doctor 7	Milliner 3	Silversmith 1	Judge 1
Blacksmith 8	Druggist 3	Minister 7	Tailor 12	Lawyer 8
Bricklayer 3	Farmer 9	Painter 4	Teacher 5	
Butcher 2	Fisherman 2	Paper Hanger 1	Tin & Iron worker 2	Editor 2
Cabinetmaker 2	Harness Maker 3	Pianist 1	Tobacconist 1	Printer 5
Carpenter 25	Machinist 1	Plasterer 1	Trader 2	
Carriagemaker 3	Mantua Maker 4	Saddler 1	Washerwoman 3	
Clerk 13	Mariner 6	Seamstress 12	Watchmaker 1	
Conveyancer 1	Merchant 20	'segar'maker (cigar) 2	Wheelwright 2	

Mantua (overskirt)

The majority of the tradespeople previously listed were men. Most woman were listed as keeping house at home. The few women who worked in a trade were seamstresses (and mantua makers), milliners and teachers. The local pianist was a woman, as of course were the washerwomen. There were three boarding house keepers in town, two of whom were women. There was also a tavern, two hotels and the jail. About 10% of these tradespeople were free blacks, with an additional seventy-five African Americans working as general laborers. These businesses made for a bustling community.

The 1860 Cambridge Census lists a population of 1,143 people [35% white males, 37% white females, 13% free black males & 15% free black females]. As the companies of the 1st Eastern Shore Volunteers gathered in town under the leadership of Colonel Wallace, the population in town would have increased significantly. Each company consisted of about one hundred men; the regiment would have totaled about a thousand. With the arrival of Brigadier General Lockwood and his troops from Delaware, the military would have outnumbered the local citizens and increased the town to more than double its former population.

"MILITARY – The steamer Pocahontas, arrived here on Saturday morning last from Wilmington, Delaware, via Perryville, Maryland with about 700 United States troops, under command of Brigadier Gen. Lockwood, and encamped near town, on the farm of Mr. T. T. Martin. They are a fine looking set of men as we have ever seen – the officers are very clever and sociable to all persons visiting camp. We shall publish a full list of the officers in our next paper."

The Cambridge Herald

"COMPANY A OF THE HOME BRIGADE – All honor to the Dorchester Guards – They are the first to enter the Home Brigade, having been sworn in on Wednesday last by Col. Wallace, thus securing the position of Company A. To accomplish this has been the ardent wish of their gallant Captain, John C. Henry, and to this end he has labored night and day recruiting his company to the required complement. We congratulate him that his efforts have been crowned with success. The company consists of about seventy-five men, with the following commissioned and non-commissioned officers:

John C. Henry, Captain

Thomas H. Coburn, First Lieutenant,

Clement T. Mowbray, Second Lieut.

William T. Robinson, First Sergeant

H. T. Winterbottom, Second Sergeant

Levin A. Dail, Third Sergeant

Levin W. Bothum, Fourth Sergeant

Philemon Geoghegan, Fifth Sergeant

Corporals – Thomas P. Snow, William Woodrow, John S. Cornwell, Orvill Mowbray, Robert B. Hubbard, William Tarr, James Straughn and Joseph H. Hudson"

The Cambridge Herald

A military camp was soon established on the east side of Cambridge Creek on the farm of Tristram Thomas Martin, of Baltimore. A search of Dorchester County Land Records shows that Mr. Martin owned one piece of property in the county at that time. Purchased December 4, 1858 from John E. and Sarah E. Stevens, "Woolford's Regulation" equaled 100 acres and consisted of all the property east of Cambridge Creek as far east as Dorchester Avenue and from the Choptank River south to Lang's Cove, near the present-day site of the Deep Harbor Condos. The camp was accessed by way of narrow footbridges across the creek. [xiii] The 1877 Cambridge Atlas shows the width of the creek was most narrow at the foot of Muir St. and the bridge was likely located there or possibly Church Street.

With the additional troops, more space was needed. The camp area may have spread south toward the head of the creek. Soon there were at least two camps in Cambridge. The Cambridge Herald frequently mentions Camp Lockwood, Camp Wharton and Camp Wallace. Though camp names appear to change, Camps Lockwood and Wharton have been named together in the local newspaper. The locations of two camps are known, but which name applied to which camp is uncertain.

The second camp was located at the head of Cambridge Creek south of present-day Cedar Street. In 1861 Cambridge Creek ran further south toward Washington Street, branching into three 'fingers'. Among these branches of the creek were meadows with a small hill. Evidence of the hill and surrounding low areas can still be seen. This area was owned by Maria Pritchard James, inherited from Dr. Arthur Bell. The property consisted of nearly a dozen acres and extended from the southeast corner of Cedar and Race Streets east to the hill where Peachblossom Avenue is today.

"Wednesday November 19, 1862

PERSONAL.---Col. Wallace, Maj. Kirby, Dr.F.P. Phelps, Chaplain Poulson, Capt. Graham and Capt. Keene, all of Colonel Wallace's regiment are in Cambridge, at this time, – we are pleased to see them all in good health. The two companies of Captains Graham, and Keene, are encamped in Cambridge, on the lot in the rear of the residence of the late Mrs. James. How long they will remain here, we are unable to say."

The Cambridge Herald

The 1877 Cambridge Atlas shows that there were few houses in the area. One building stands alone on the hill, unidentified. It is believed that this one room, single-story building was built at the time of the encampments. In later years the head of the creek would be partially filled in for the extension of Cedar Street. The area around the hill was divided into lots. The 'camp fort' became the kitchen portion of a family home on Peachblossom Avenue. Though the kitchen wing has since been replaced, an old well on the property may be the only surviving relic of the Union camp.

The Cambridge Herald frequently mentioned the local troops in their weekly publication. These brief articles give us a first-hand glimpse of life in the Federal camps. Besides the obvious necessity of drilling and maintaining the camp, there were flag raisings and parades through town accompanied by the Company Band. There was a fifty foot high flagpole raised in front of Colonel Wallace's headquarters. The local citizens were welcomed on frequent visits and Sundays were occasions for sermons and singing. A member of Co. E from Preston, Caroline County wrote in a Letter to the Editor:

"*Preston Company, Sept. 29, 1861*

Mr. Editor – We had the pleasure this afternoon, of hearing a sermon by the Rev. Mr. Numbers, Captain of the Preston Company; who did enlist to himself, and the regiment in which we are enlisted. The speaker's stand was located beneath the stars and stripes, the glorious emblem of our nationality; which floated from a pole some fifty feet high; in front of Col. Wallace's headquarters. Before the Reverend gentleman commenced his remarks, the different companies of our camp were marched by their respective commanders around the stand; after which the exercises of the afternoon commenced with singing and prayer by our christian solders; who in the language of General McClellan, formed the regiment to give his body to his country, and his soul to his God. After the sermon, the companies immediately appeared on dress parade; commanded by our worthy Colonel and assisted by Adjt. Rastall, whose gentlemanly deportment, and (?) military capacities, render him highly popular with all persons under his command. We hope Mr. Editor, that you will excuse this short, but well lined letter, as it is written amidst the noise and hustle of military life. With a trunk for a seat, a dry goods box for a table, and a candle without a candlestick; with our ears listening to a hundred different sounds; of singing, of laughing, and all kinds of discord imaginable, we are writing this communication. The noise and confusion is so great in our tent, that we are compelled to quit writing.

Calvert"

from The Cambridge Herald

With so much activity between the camps and town, it was necessary to construct additional footbridges over the several branches and guts of the creek. These bridges were apparently built by the property owners for the use of Federal troops and local citizens. One citizen objected to the bridge 'situation' and expressed his displeasure in a Letter to the Editor:

"Mr. Editor – I desire through your excellent Paper to call the attention of the citizens of Cambridge, and more particularly the officers of Camps Wharton & Lockwood to the gross and shameful imposition practiced on our citizens daily by the "shylocks" that pretend to be the proprietors of the Bridges that cross our creek to the above camps. Now if I understand the matter correctly, the pretended owners of the Bridges actually charged the officers of the above camps the sum of thirty Dollars apiece for the construction of the above Bridges which is about twice the cost of the same, for if the material is used six months, it will be worth almost as much as it was the day they were laid, therefore, the material cost almost nothing. The loose and unsafe manner the Bridges are laid, make the cost of construction, but trifling. But in addition to the enormous price paid for the Bridges, these Rebel shylocks are allowed to collect toll to the tune of two cents for every individual that crosses. In justice to the citizens of the Town and County, the officers of the above camps ought to stop the collection of tolls on the Bridges.

Justice."

The Cambridge Herald

Chapter Three
Duty and Service

For over two months the town of Cambridge was bustling with military activity. On November 11, 1861 Brigadier General Lockwood received orders from Baltimore to proceed to Accomack and Northampton Counties in Virginia and establish control of the area on behalf of the United States. Military occupation of the Eastern Shore of Virginia was deemed necessary for several reasons. First and foremost, the presence of Rebel troops on the Delmarva Peninsula was a potential threat to the entire Shore. If the Confederate Army had sent troops across the lower Chesapeake Bay, they might have attempted an invasion into the North via the Eastern Shore. It was therefore advisable to hold the Lower Shore under Federal control. The plan was that the Rebel companies of Eastern Virginia be arrested. Further contact with mainland Virginia would be forbidden. Citizens would be free to continue as usual, provided they cooperated with Lockwood's forces. This meant the arrest of anyone smuggling supplies or information to the enemy. There was to be no harm to personal property during the occupation. A proclamation to that effect was sent to Accomack and Northampton Counties ahead of the invasion:

"To the People of Accomac and Northampton Co.s, Va:

The military forces of the United States are about to enter your counties as a part of the Union. They will go among you as friends, and with the earnest hope that they may not, by your own acts, be forced to become your enemies. They will invade no rights of person or property; on the contrary, your laws, your institutions, and your usages, will be scrupulously respected. There need be no fear that the quietude of any fireside will be disturbed, unless disturbance is caused by yourselves....."

The Cambridge Herald

Once Federal troops gained control of Eastern Virginia, one important task was to patrol the east coast of the Chesapeake Bay and hinder blockade runners. Many southern sympathizers throughout the Delmarva Peninsula smuggled letters, food and supplies to their family members in the South. Some rebels, rather than join the Southern Army, contributed to The Cause by transporting goods across the Chesapeake Bay to mainland Virginia. Small boats with dark sails would hide in the numerous coves and inlets along the coast. After dark they would set sail for Virginia, hoping to elude detection and capture. Another kind of cargo was also transported; young men headed for enlistment into the Confederate Army. Many young men throughout the peninsula left home secretly and traveled along the 'underground railroad' south, hiding during the day in marshes along the shore. At the appointed time they would meet a captain of a small boat ready to transport them across the bay for a price. Running the blockade provided a tidy income, though the risk of capture and arrest was great.

At the time of the above proclamation, the Eastern Shore of Virginia was a part of the Confederacy in spite of its separation from mainland Virginia by the Chesapeake Bay. Eastern Virginia consisted of two counties, Accomack County to the north and Northampton County to the south at the southern tip of the Delmarva Peninsula. As part of Confederate Virginia, one would expect strong southern sympathies in the citizens of both counties and this was true for Northampton County. However, communities further north into Accomack were of mixed opinions. Allegiance to the United States was found to be more prevalent the closer one approached the Maryland / Virginia line, though there were still a large number of citizens who supported the Southern Cause.

Rebel troops had been organizing in the area for some time. As Lockwood's brigade prepared to invade Eastern Virginia, the Virginia troops readied to meet that inevitable invasion. The 39th Regiment of Volunteers under Colonel Charles Smith was stationed near the Maryland / Virginia line and consisted of eight companies of Infantry and two companies of Cavalry, as well as a company of Light Artillery. The 39th Regiment would later become the 39th Virginia Infantry, C.S. The men of Colonel Smith's command were joined by the 2nd Regiment of Militia which included two Rifle companies, the Accomack Rifles and the Onancock Rifles, and a company of Artillery. These men were commanded by Colonel Gunter. The various camps established at that time included camps near Oak Hall, Evergreen Farm on the south side of Pungoteague Creek, Rural Felicity Farm near Drummondtown (now known as Accomac, Va.[xiv]), Jenkins Bridge in Upper Accomack County, and Harper's Ferry in Accomack County near Grangeville.[xv]

The troops of Eastern Virginia prepared their defenses by burning bridges to slow the progress of the approaching Northern troops and building breastworks that would provide cover when under fire. Earlier in August the 39th Regiment had exchanged gunfire with Union troops from Fortress Monroe.[xvi] Those troops from Ft. Monroe had sailed across the Chesapeake Bay and landed near Cherrystone Creek. After three hours of exchanging gunfire, the North finally withdrew. No lives were lost on either side.

The 39th and 2nd Regiments, C.S., numbering between 1,500 and 2,000 men, converged near the Maryland / Virginia line. A line of breastworks was established one mile south of New Church along present-day Route 13. An additional force was sent north toward the state line, where they set up pickets at the Pitts Creek Bridge. The men camped on the farm of John Brittingham for nearly two weeks in anticipation of a confrontation with Federal troops. The Brittingham family supported the Southern Cause. However, John was concerned about exposing his family to the dangers of the battle that was threatening to occur in his own front yard. In order to protect his family as much as possible, John asked his brother-in-law Samuel C. Jones of Newtown, Maryland (now known as Pocomoke[xvii]) to let him know when the Union troops were near.

November 15, 1861 Brig. Gen. Lockwood sent a man named Dickinson over the state line into Virginia under a flag of truce. Dickinson's assignment was to distribute copies of Lockwood's proclamation which assured the Virginians of their non-violent intent, as long as the local citizens cooperated. That night Sam Jones arrived at the Brittingham farm to alert John that the Federal invasion was eminent. His message was overheard by some of the officers of the 39th and 2nd Regiments who were sleeping in the Brittingham's front room.

Learning that they were vastly outnumbered and would be facing over 5,000 Federal troops, more than double their own number, the decision was made to retreat. A confrontation at that time would surely have been a disaster for the Virginia troops. Some returned to their homes and others retreated south hoping to cross the

Bay and join up with Confederate troops on the mainland. Over the ensuing weeks, many men of Eastern Virginia quietly did just that and were able to continue proudly fighting for the Southern Cause.[xviii]

Meanwhile, the Union troops had gathered in Newtown, Maryland (Pocomoke) in preparation for the invasion. Six companies of the 5th New York Volunteer Infantry, U.S. had left Baltimore on November 12 on the steamer Pocahontas heading for Newtown. The 4th Wisconsin Infantry under Colonel Halbert Payne, the 6th Michigan Infantry and the 21st Indiana Infantry under Colonel James W. McMillan also headed to Newtown where they were joined by Colonel Wallace's 1st Eastern Shore Volunteers and the 2nd Delaware Infantry recently from Cambridge. The entire invading force was commanded by Brig. Gen. Henry H. Lockwood, of Delaware. Part of the 4th Wisconsin and an additional troop of Cavalry had landed earlier at Whitehaven, on the Wicomico River. From there they marched east to Princess Anne and on to Snow Hill before joining Lockwood in Newtown.

Marching toward the Maryland / Virginia line, Lockwood's cavalry led the way into Eastern Virginia. They met no military resistance upon arrival. The Rebel troops had dispersed, leaving behind breastworks, burned bridges and blockaded roads. The men themselves had either left for the Virginia mainland to join the Confederate Army or returned to their homes. Lockwood established a camp at Drummondtown, the county seat of Accomack County, which is today known as Accomac, Va. In Drummondtown, Lockwood claimed the Episcopal Rectory as his headquarters. The Drummondtown Methodist Church became the barracks and the Mackemie Presbyterian Church was used to stable troop horses. With their churches in use by the invading Union army, citizens resorted to gathering in the Court House or private homes for worship.

Other camps were setup as needed throughout Eastern Virginia including Camp Blair located near Eastville, Northampton County, on Hungers Creek and Camp Cherrystone near Townsfield. The Rebel camp on Rural Felicity Farm, near Drummondtown, had been abandoned with the invasion of Union troops. The 2nd Delaware established their camp on that site and named it Camp Wilkes.

Though the occupation of the Lower Delmarva was relatively peaceful, the citizens still maintained a quiet loyalty to the Confederacy. Blockade runners were a constant concern, smuggling supplies and information across the Chesapeake Bay. This would have been the only contact families could have with their loved ones serving in the Southern Army. Trade between troops and the local citizenry was strictly monitored and any suspicious 'secesh'[xix] activity was investigated.

Another reason that occupation of the Lower Shore was an important strategy was the telegraph line. Dispatches from Union-held Fortress Monroe on the Virginia mainland had to go by boat up the Bay to Annapolis and then by telegraph to Washington. With the Delmarva Peninsula securely in the possession of the Union Army, a telegraph line was laid from Wilmington, Delaware to Cherrystone, Virginia. In a short time additional cable was laid along the bed of the Bay, connecting Cherrystone to Hampton Roads, Virginia. This enabled officers at Fortress Monroe to telegraph dispatches across the Bay to Cherrystone and up the peninsula, providing efficient and secure passage of information to Washington. [xx]

In addition to maintaining a watchful eye for secessionist activities, guarding the telegraph line was a primary duty. The underwater line was in constant danger of breaking. If the waves and weather conditions did not break communications, Rebels did. In the summer of 1862 the cable was cut preventing General McClellan from relaying important dispatches to Washington. Forced to find other means of communication, the General came discreetly ashore with a few men in civilian attire and surprised a telegraph operator at Townsville, Virginia. They spent a number of hours in communication with Washington, causing much excitement the following morning among the local soldiers. [xxi]

Once the Lower Shore was secure, the out-of-state troops relocated to different posts and many of the Delmarva troops were sent to establish camps in other areas of the Peninsula. Lockwood's main headquarters was moved from Cambridge to Salisbury, being more centrally located and closer to the recently constructed railroad which ran from Wilmington to Salisbury. Camp Wallace (aka Camp Upton) was established on the rise of land south of Humphreys Lake, currently the site of the Times Building, near the Salisbury Hospital. Most of the Delmarva camps were occupied by infantry and a few cavalry companies. Camp Upton however did have some small number of artillery positioned to strike at strategic points in the event that defense was required.

Additional camps were located in most of the primary towns on the Shore. Camps in Princess Anne and Newtown were named Bradford Barracks and Camp Halleck, respectively. Camp Pocahontas was located in Eastville, Virginia. A Camp Quaker has been noted both near Trappe and on the grounds of the Third Haven Meeting House near Easton. Troops also visited many other towns throughout the Peninsula. Companies patrolled through the camps regularly, camping for a few days or weeks and then marching on to another location. From period photos taken in other regions, it can be assumed that most camps would have consisted primarily of tents. Use would have been made of unused buildings and even public buildings in the vicinity. In winter, tents might have been surrounded by log walls built to help keep out the cold. In some cases, buildings may have been built specifically for camp use. [xxii] When troops were on the move, it is likely they took shelter wherever they could find it.

"CAMP KIRBY, near Easton, Md.

January 27, 1862

Mr. Editor: – The weekly issues of your valuable paper reaches our camp regularly, and always is greeted with smiles by your numerous friends in the detachments, situated near Easton. Presuming that a few lines from one who has so lately been encamped near your town, might be interesting to you, and your readers, I assume the responsibility of addressing you this communication.

Camp Kirby is situated in a thick, heavy forest, near the town of Easton, and is securely protected from the cold blasts of winter by the surrounding woods. Our Winter Quarters are now in the course of erection and when completed our little camp will compare with that of any regiment in the service. The buildings for the use of each company will be nearly a hundred feet by fifteen feet. This building, with the exception of sixteen feet used for a kitchen, is to be divided into ten apartments, into each of which will be quartered eight men.

Our detachment under command of Major Kirby is enjoying excellent health, but few being in the hospital at the present. It may be remarked here that the weather has been very unfavorable to the health of the troops, but yet our sick list is very small indeed. The cases reported are not at all dangerous, but three being confined to their beds. Our hospital is for the present situated in the town of Easton, in the building occupied by Mr. Wallaston , the proprietor of the "Union Hotel". This gentleman deserves great praise for the kindness which he has shown to our sick, who have in a manner been under his care. This treatment to the sick gains him many friends in our detachment. He is loved and respected by all. From this building, now floats the "Banner of the Free", the only one raised in the town of Easton, for many months.

The reception of troops in this town presents a striking contrast to that in the town of Cambridge. Instead of the cheerful countenance and the friendly smile with which a soldier was treated in your town, we now generally receive the cold stern look of the residents of Easton. 'Tis true as in all other matters, there are to be found some exceptions to the above. One gentleman, in truth his whole household, who is to be particularly mentioned as an exception to the above remark, is Mr. Edward Woodall, whose residence is near our camp. In him we have found a true friend, both to us and the cause in which we are engaged. When first we encamp(ed) in his woods, many inconveniences would we have been troubled with had it not been for the kindness shown us by this gentleman, for his kind actions towards us he receives our most sincere thanks.

This communication is written under all the inconveniences of Camp life. In one place we hear the strains of some national air and at the same time we hear the tap of the drum. Many are the interruptions a person receives while writing a few lines. Hoping that this may be some apology for the many inaccuracies in my letter, I will bring this communication to a close. You may in some future day receive another from your friend in CAMP KIRBY"

The Cambridge Herald

Camp Kirby was located on the farm of Edward Woodall near Easton. The Woodall family, from Little Creek Hundred, Kent County, Delaware purchased the property on Dover Road in 1858 from Theodore Denny. The site is now occupied by the Clifton Industrial Park. Camp Kirby maintained a Union presence in Easton, a town with much sympathy for the Southern Cause. In addition, during the Draft of 1862, all draftees on the Eastern Shore reported to Camp Kirby for processing and orientation. From there they were shipped out on steamboats to their respective assignments.

Service in the Home Guard consisted of drills and picket duty as well as guarding the aforementioned telegraph line. Companies patrolled from camp to camp, ever watchful of 'secesh' activities. Occasionally they were called upon to confiscate arms or arrest a citizen for smuggling or speaking out against the Union. Each occupied town flew a Union flag. Though many citizens fully supported the Union cause, there were others who did not. Some were apt to go out of their way to avoid walking under the Union flag, in protest of the military occupation. One such young woman was Clara Gunby of Salisbury. Miss Gunby refused to walk beneath "that Yankee flag". Her defiance led to her arrest and detainment at Fortress Monroe where she met another prisoner who had been arrested as a spy. Clara was eventually exiled to Richmond, where she carried a message to President Jefferson Davis from the spy she met at Ft. Monroe. She lived in Richmond for the remainder of the war.

Letters from family and friends were a precious connection with life back home. Members of the Home Guard were fortunate to be stationed closer to home than most soldiers. Perhaps that accounts for the lack of letters surviving today. Letters home can provide personal glimpses of life in camp and one such collection of letters comes from Lt. Adjutant John E. Rastall of Milwaukee, Wisconsin[xxiii]. Rastall was assigned to the 1st Eastern Shore Md. Volunteers early in the War. His frequent letters home illustrate the time and place in a way that history books cannot.

"Feb. 8, 1862 .....here (Salisbury) *the children have a practice of hurrahing for Jeff.* [xxiv] *and their parents smile.... every day almost we hear a heavy cannonade on the Potomac, but can't tell what it means.... it is very hard to get correct reports, our regiment is so distant and split up, little detachments here and there, all have to come in to make it correct...."*

"March 15, 1862 (New Castle, Del.) *.... it is necessary for me to stay with the men in their barracks. Our men are in an old R R machine shop too old for use and we sleep on the ground. This nice arrangement saves me 50 cents a day for bed. The nights are cold but we huddle together – the officers of the companies – and keep warm. As I sit here writing we have just received an order from Col. to have 2 companies ready to move at 3 o'clock Co's K & C. I am ordered to command Company K, 80 men strong, the Captain being sick. It is now 10 o'clock so I must hurry..... Plenty of game and shellfish. While in Salisbury, we fed our men on oysters in lieu of fresh meat, they are to be found in all the rivers and bays of this county."*

"May 2, 1862 ....(Drummondtown) I have been ordered into camp Drummond and have my office in an old log pine shanty, which leaks like fury. Last night I awoke with the water dropping on my face from a hole in the roof. Got up, put my oil cloth over my desk and papers and then covered myself up and slept sound till morning. Woke, built a fire, dried my clothes and was all O. K. Going to stretch my tent over the

outside roof and nail it down, shall keep dry then....Haven't got home sick yet except an occasional attack on a wet night or when provisions run short. The fish season is about due and hundreds are caught per day by a single line in the inlet – Metomkin. Some very large fish. Am collecting some rare curiosities for you from the beach. Star fish, conk spawn, shell, no such thing as starvation here in the summer. Our men have been attacked by scurvy a good deal in the winter but now fresh meat is obtained and it is fast disappearing. One company was afflicted with the "itch" and we nick-named it the "company in active service". Warm weather is just coming on. I dread it but the sea beach is near and bathing will be very acceptable if we remain..... "

"May 18, 1862 ... the encampment is to be pitched near the barracks we now occupy. I have had my tent thoroughly overhauled, cleaned and am going to repair it tomorrow. I am living extremely economical now, paying but little for board and buying nothing. My clothes look the worst for wear alongside that of the other officers and I sent to Baltimore for a new suit, but the person I sent by lost the measure and I am not sorry for it as I am about $40 richer by the operation. I shall have my old clothes cleaned, buy some new buttons put on my new shoulder straps and I think that will have to last awhile yet. The good clothes ware out by having to put them on each day for dress parade, and mine have to go on (&) off. I keep a good suit – twice, once at guard in the morning and at the evening parade. So that instead of changing twice a day, I wear the clothes I have all the time. ..."

"May 25, 1862 ....(Drummondtown, Va.) *It is astonishing how much money we have to pay out for clothing. Living near town and three or four of the officers having their families with them we have to keep up a pretty respectable appearance. It would be different if we were in the field, but as it is we are now living the same as at home, surrounded by everyone the same as yourselves. The camp is nicely located near the woods to the right of the barracks we have been in during the spring and trees have been set out between the pretty white streets, gardens made ornamental with shells and the camp frequented*

by a great number. The summer has set in though it is very warm here, still the sea breezes will make the air cool and comfortable. I hear that this spot is frequently visited by hurricanes, which will play the mischief with our tents. The health of the camp is excellent and combining this with good wholesome discipline, the men keep in good spirits and are very comfortable. In the army as I suppose you are aware, we examine the men's clothing once a week to see if they keep themselves clean, the Colonel being very strict in this respect – for it is essential to health. I have seen him several times order the men from the ranks and detail a sergeant and a couple of men to take the poor fellow down and wash him, and they do it....."

"July 31, 1862 .... (Eastville, Va.) *We have several officers taking an inventory of Rebel Estates to meet the Confiscation Act....We took 300 sheep on one Island and in pursuance to orders gave a receipt for them. We have orders to this effect and shall never run short of fresh meat or vegetables again.*

I am in a perfect state as usual and the best health. Father's "envelope" letter came to hand. Write as often as I do.

Love to all. Jack" [xxv]

Another Union camp was Camp Halleck in Newtown, Maryland, now called Pocomoke. With soldiers living in close quarters, with an often limited food supplies, health was a concern. Early in their service there was an wave of measles through many of the camps and some of the soldiers died.

"CAMP HALLECK

Newtown, March 4, 1862

"Mr. Editor – Having seen an invitation in the Herald, requesting a correspondence from the different camps of Colonel Wallace's regiment, I am thus prompted to

obtrude myself upon you, whilst I attempt to chronicle a few lines, relative to this detachment, and its vicinity. We have two companies, C & D commanded respectfully by Captains Comegys & Stafford; and numbering in all 141 men, who have been stationed here since the 7th of last December, after a sojourn of eighteen days in the State of poor old Virginia. We are comfortably quartered in board tents, 14 by 16 feet, and located on the east bank of the Pocomoke River, thirty miles from its mouth, and sixteen miles below Snow Hill; five miles from the Virginia line, and only two miles from where the rebel pickets were posted when our troops arrived at this place, on the 14th of November last....

The health of our sick has much improved since we "used up" the measles, which prevailed to an alarming extent, six weeks ago. The hospital is in charge of Dr. McMaster, of Newtown; and doubtless under his skillful treatment, the afflicted will soon recover. Newtown has a population of 800 inhabitants, with five churches, four schools, six dry-goods houses, two hotels, and a post-office; besides a number of handsome private residences. The Union feeling is very strong in this section and furnishes a pleasing contrast to the rebel sentiment which your correspondent from Camp Kirby speaks of as prevailing in Easton.

Before I close, I must not neglect to mention the great kindness, bestowed upon our sick men by the citizens of this town, and especially have the ladies manifested an almost overwhelming hospitality, toward the sick, since our sojourn in this locality. This is truly characteristic of these of the fair sex, who have nobly espoused that cause, which still upholds the proud and starry symbol, of an indivisible nationality.

Richard"

The Cambridge Herald

Chapter Four
Company A
1st Eastern Shore Maryland Volunteers

With the Eastern Shore of Virginia securely occupied and under the control of the Union Army, the Delmarva troops maintained their patrols throughout the Peninsula until the Spring of 1863. The pending invasion of Confederate troops into Western Maryland and Pennsylvania prompted the Army of the Potomac to call for all available troops to converge on the Western Shore of Maryland in defense. Delmarva troops reported to Baltimore and were sent west toward Frederick, Maryland. Near Cookesville a detachment of the 1st Eastern Shore Infantry clashed briefly with the cavalry troops of J.E.B. Stuart [xxvi], who was on his way to meet General Robert E. Lee [xxvii]. Following the skirmish at Cookesville, the 1st E. S. Infantry continued their march toward Taneytown, Md.

J.E.B. Stuart and his cavalrymen headed off toward Westminster, Md. There they encountered Companies A and C of the 1st Delaware Cavalry under Major Napoleon Bonaparte Knight [xxviii], who after a brief time on the Delmarva Peninsula, had been posted there to defend the railway line, assisted by a small guard of the 150th New York Infantry. When a scout brought news of Stuart's approach, Major Knight was occupied at a local tavern. With no time for delay, Captain Charles Corbit of Company C gathered his men and led a daring charge against the enemy. A violent battle ensued at the corner of Main and Washington Streets. Captain Corbit's men were greatly outnumbered and most were captured and later paroled. However, their actions delayed Stuart's march by half a day. Major Knight escaped with approximately 28 men and Stuart continued his march toward Pennsylvania, joining up with General Lee at Gettysburg. One might wonder if the Confederate losses at Gettysburg might have been in part due to Stuart's delay at Cooksville and Westminster. Though Stuart's encounters with Delmarva troops were relatively minor, his delayed arrival at Gettysburg left General Lee without crucial information about the 'lay of the land' and the location of the enemy, information that Stuart's Cavalry would have provided. The 1st Eastern Shore Infantry continued on to Gettysburg, arriving the evening of the second day of battle. The following morning, they were sent to re-enforce troops from Pennsylvania on Culp's Hill. Here they successfully defended against the 1st (later renamed 2nd) Maryland Infantry, C.S. Many of the 1st / 2nd Maryland, C.S. were men from the Eastern Shore who had left for Richmond. The 1st Eastern Shore Regiment losses included 7 men killed, 22 wounded and 7 missing. The 1st / 2nd Maryland, C.S. lost nearly half their men in the three days of the Battle of Gettysburg.

One company of the 1st Eastern Shore was not present on Culp's Hill that day. Company A, under the leadership of Captain John C. Henry had been discharged the previous summer, having served only eleven months of their three year enlistment. Enlistment began September 11, 1861 with thirty eight men signing up in Cambridge. According to military records, seven were recruited in East New Market, three in St. Michaels and one each in Federalsburg and Vienna on the same day. J. C. Henry is credited with most of the enlistments. Over the next two weeks, twelve more enlisted, most in Cambridge. Beginning September 24th Captain Henry recruited nineteen more men in St. Michaels in the course of a week. During the month of October another dozen men enlisted in Dorchester County, with three late-comers joining the company that winter.[xxix]

Capt. John C. Henry, of Cambridge was elected Captain by his fellow soldiers soon after enlistment. He was assisted in his command by 1st Lt. Thomas H. Coburn and 2nd Lt. Clement T. Mowbray. Their command consisted of about a hundred men. Most were from Dorchester County, though at least one was from Somerset County, one from Baltimore City and nearly two dozen were from Talbot County. Little is known of the men of Company A. Census and pension records shed some light on the lives of these men, but for many we have only their names on enlistment records. From the information available the majority were in their 20's. The youngest appears to have been William Henry Haddaway who enlisted in Talbot County at the age of 17. Hugh C. Bennett was probably the oldest of the group, being 45 years old at the time of his enlistment in Cambridge. The soldiers' occupations at the beginning of the War reflect the communities they lived in. Most were farmers, but others were carpenters or laborers. Many worked on or around the bay, catching fish and oysters, or working as mariners and sailors. There were four sets of brothers in Company A: Charles and John Cummings and Daniel and John Haddaway of Talbot County; George and Levin Dail and Hooper and Joseph Smith from Dorchester County.

In November 1861 Brig. General Lockwood received orders to lead his brigade south and establish control of the Eastern Shore of Virginia. The various troops headed south, some passing through Snow Hill and Princess Anne and all gathering in Newtown (Pocomoke), just north of the Maryland / Virginia line. As many of the troops headed down into Virginia by land, the men of

Company A were sent by a different route. Leaving Newtown Sergeant Bothum had this to say:

"Our detachment of troops was put aboard two schooners and towed down the river [Pocomoke River] *by the steamer Balloon. Opposite Watt Island* [xxx] *in the Chesapeake Bay the two vessels and steamboat ran aground on the shoals out there and laid there all night, and if the wind had blown hard we should have had a rough time of it out there. Next morning we were towed off up to Chesconnessex Wharf but we did not go ashore until next morning, when our detachment pitched their tents in the woods. While we were aboard the vessels we had a disagreeable time of it. Raining and nothing to eat, we stayed in the woods two or three days, and then marched to Drummondtown, eight miles from our camp. When we got there we pitched our tents in (a) potato patch. The rebels of Eastern Virginia left the country or dispersed before we got here. We stayed in Drummondtown until next morning when we moved out about two miles from town. We camped there about three weeks and had very little rations. We lived on sweet potatoes while we were there. From there we marched to Newtown in Maryland. It was about 30 miles. It took us about two days to march it and we stayed there four days. Our company was ordered to Princess Anne, one day's march, 16 miles. A few days after we arrived there we proceeded to put up winter quarters, and we got into them about Christmas. Our duty was light. We had to guard the telegraph line from Princess Anne half way to Salisbury, and we drilled all good days while we were there.*

"Sometime in March of 1862 we were ordered up in Delaware. We went to New Castle and barracked in a machine shop. And, from there,we went to Delaware City and got some arms. Stayed there a few days and went

back to New Castle, and from there went back to Salisbury. We marched back to Princess Anne in the night, got back to our quarters about 9 o'clock at night. We stayed in our winter quarters until April, when we were ordered to Newtown again. In a few days we were ordered on the Telegraph line that connected Washington with Fortress Monroe, which was the base of operation for the Army of the Potomac. Our duty was to guard the line from Princess Anne to New Church, Va., distance 25 miles – ten men at a station, 2 ½ miles apart, Duty light, plenty (to) eat, and we had a jolly time of it, generally. My station was down in Virginia about 1 ½ miles over the line of Md. We guarded the telegraph line until about 16(th) of August when we were ordered down in Va."

Sergeant Levin W. Bothum[xxxi]

We can learn much from the few paragraphs written by Bothum. Though he did not state who else took the 'Chesconnessex Route', it is likely that at least one other company went along. Co. A had traveled from Cambridge to Newtown on the steamer Balloon with part of the 2nd Delaware. Though schooners varied in size, many schooners could probably hold about one company. Company A was in fact crowded aboard a schooner the following year. Thus the two schooners might be expected to hold two companies. More troops may have traveled aboard the steamer, though this is unknown. The troops that accompanied Capt. Henry's men may have been some of the 2nd Delaware, but were more likely of the 1st Eastern Shore, as they would be more experienced on The Bay. The steamer's ability to tow the schooners would be invaluable as calm weather could leave sail boats adrift with no power to navigate.

The purpose of sending troops along this route was a point of strategy. The main body of troops invaded Eastern Virginia by land, crossing the Maryland / Virginia border near where Rt. 13 runs today. The Chesconnessex group, landing further south in Virginia and meeting the main body at Drummondtown would have the opportunity of either a surprise strike to the enemy's flank while they were engaged with the Union troops, or an ambush should the enemy retreat.

Their journey began in Newtown on the Pocomoke River. Twenty-some miles down the Pocomoke River they entered Pocomoke Sound, a bay that empties into the Chesapeake Bay. Boating into The Bay they would have headed south, between Tangier Island and Eastern Virginia. The shoals off Beach Island, west of Big Marsh, Virginia is directly opposite Watts Island. It was here that the boats ran aground. They apparently waited the night for the rising tide to allow them to continue on their mission. The weather in November can vary. Bothum describes it as cold and rainy. Their lack of supplies would indicate their intention of a quick direct trip south, now complicated by the delay off Beach Island.

It is interesting to note the lack of supplies during this early stage of occupation. It is supposed that once camps were established and secure, attention was given to obtaining food for the troops. As with the majority of residents on the Shore, the primary diet may have been fish or oysters, being readily available. Once the Confiscation Act was enacted, foodstuffs seized from known Rebels and blockade runners could be used by the army.

The weather must have continued with little wind, as the schooners were towed on to Chesconnessex Creek and up to the public wharf on the northern bank. Today

Chesconnessex Wharf is a small village made up of a single road lined with older homes. The appearance of some of the houses suggest they might have been there at the time of the Union invasion. South Chesconnessex lies across the creek to the south. A browse through the 1860 census for the Onancock area, of which Chesconnessex is a part, reveals that the large majority of the rural population of the area was made up of sailors, watermen and oystermen, with livelihoods strongly dependent on the Chesapeake Bay's bounty.

Bothum relates that after disembarking from the schooners at Chesconnessex Wharf, they pitched their tents and camped in the woods nearby, staying a couple of days before marching on to Drummondtown. If they brought no food supplies with them, they likely had used up what little fresh water they had brought along. Though the families living nearby might well have spared food and fresh water for the men of Company A, the reminder that they were in enemy territory might have made the men reluctant to trust the local citizens. Further, rebels in the area might prevent them from joining the main body of troops at Drummondtown. At it turned out, enemy troops had been so out-numbered by the main body of Union troops that they had retreated south, soon to leave the Delmarva Peninsula for Richmond.

After a brief camp in the woods Capt. Henry and his men marched to Drummondtown, setting up camp in a potato patch a couple of miles from town. Accounts from pension records recall the weather as cold with a mix of snow and rain, uncomfortable sleeping on the bare ground. With so little food available, they lived off the sweet potatoes dug from the field in which they were camped. That potato patch is long gone, but a study of a map of the area may suggest a possible campsite. Of the few roads leading into town, the two leading south might be the most likely to bring rebel soldiers within their lines. Drummondtown Road toward Locustville and the current Rt. 13 are both roads that would have needed guarding. About a mile south on Drummondtown Rd. lies a farm called Rural Felicity, the site of Camp Wilkes of the 2nd Delaware Infantry during the winter of 1861-2. This regiment would have been positioned to intercept any Rebel invasion from this direction. The second road, running near where Rt. 13 runs today, would have been another thoroughfare that required guard against Rebels from the south. The intersection of Rt. 316 and Tasley Rd. is directly on the route between Chesconnessex and Drummondtown, and is about two miles from Drummondtown. The sweet potato patch might well have been in this rough vicinity.

After three weeks camped near Drummondtown, Company A marched a couple of days to Newtown in Maryland. They stayed there a few days and then continued on to Princess Anne. As with the sweet potato patch camp, the locations of Camp Halleck in Newtown and Bradford Barracks in Princess Anne are not known. One source places Camp Halleck on Clarke Ave., along the Pocomoke River in Newtown. [xxxii] Once in Princess Anne, the company proceed to setup a winter camp. This would become their main base of operations, though the companies of the 1st E. S. Md. Volunteers, including Company A moved around regularly.

Company A spent time in Eastern Virginia, and much time in Princess Anne and Newtown, in addition to a foray into Delaware. Sergeant Bothum describes one of their main assignments guarding the telegraph line. Ten men were stationed at each station, 2 ½ miles apart, stretching from Princess Anne, Maryland into Eastern Virginia. In March of 1862 they were sent to New Castle,

Delaware and onto Delaware City during which they confiscated arms from suspected secessionists.

According to Sergeant Bothum's personal account written after the War, in late July of 1862 he and two fellow soldiers were on leave. Bothum stayed with his uncle at Upper Trappe (present-day Eden), just south of Salisbury. Orderly Sgt. Harrison T. Winterbottom and 3rd Sgt. Levin H. Dail were returning from a visit home in Cambridge. The three men first returned to Bradford Barracks in Princess Anne where Company A had been stationed. They stayed the night in camp and left the following morning for Newtown. They spent the night in Newtown with Robert Marshall, a hotel keeper, who took them next morning on the last leg of their journey to meet up with their company.

At the time, Company A was on a schooner on the Pocomoke River opposite Shelltown, Md. According to Bothum, the ship was stopped at the Maryland / Virginia line. When the men joined their company on the schooner, Captain Henry and a squad of about 16 men had left the boat for Drummondtown, Va. The rest of the men spent about a week on the boat and upon the squad's return, they left for Newtown "*and after some delay were discharged from service by order of Gen. Wool, the commander of the Middle Department, on Aug. 16, 1862.*" [xxxiii]

So ended the service of Company A after only eleven months.

National Archives, Washington, D.C.

OCT. 15. 13256132 1891

CERTIFICATE OF MUSTERING OFFICER.

I CERTIFY, ON HONOR, That I have at ...., on this .... day of ...., 186 ..., carefully examined this Roll, and, as far as practicable, caused the allowances, stoppages, and remarks to be justly and properly stated, and mustered the company for discharge; and it is hereby honorably discharged from the service of the United States ....

.... Brig Genl

.... *Mustering Officer.*

Muster: { Station .... Date of ....

General Notation: ....

(479) *Copyist.*

National Archives, Washington, D.C.

Co. A. 1st Eastern Shore Maryland Infty.

GENERAL NOTATION.

Book mark: R. & P. 433766

Record and Pension Office,

WAR DEPARTMENT,

Washington, Jan. 10, 1896

This company was mustered out of service for refusing to obey orders, Aug. 16. 1862, in accordance with special instructions of Maj. Genl. Wool of Aug. 6 & 12, 1862, and the members so mustered out are regarded by this Department as having been discharged without honor.

Chapter Five
Early Discharge

The 1st Eastern Shore Maryland Volunteers began enlistment in September 1861 in Cambridge, Maryland. According to the announcement in the Cambridge Herald *"the Secretary of War expressly pledges that they 'shall be stationed on the Eastern Shore of Maryland' and used only for 'Home Protection' ..... The time of enlistment will be three years, or until the end of the War.... "* Company A was honorably discharged in August 1862, after only eleven months.

Thirty years later, the Pension Act of 1890 brought about revisions by the Pension Commission. One such change was that an Honorable Discharge was necessary in order to receive a pension. As the Commission began reviewing existing pension cases and new applications, the circumstances of Company A caught their attention. On January 10, 1896 a General Notation of the Record and Pension Office, War Department states *"This company was mustered out of service for refusing to obey orders, Aug. 16, 1862, in accordance with special instructions of Maj. Genl. Wool of Aug. 6 and 12, 1862 and the members so mustered out are regarded by this Department as having been discharged without honor."* [xxxiv] While members of Company A who re-enlisted with other regiments were eligible for pension by virtue of their service in those other regiments, the men who were mustered out of Company A and did not re-enlist could no longer receive a pension. Many veterans and their families lost financial assistance as a result.

The cause for this change of status from "honorable" to "without honor" is due to the apparent disobedience of an order to go into Eastern Virginia, though details are scarce. As seen in the enlistment agreement announced in the local newspapers, the regiment was clearly intended to remain on the Eastern Shore of Maryland. Yet by all accounts, the companies of the regiment went into Eastern Virginia and Delaware on several occasions. After the initial invasion of Accomac and Northampton Counties of Virginia, many companies spent time in the area on patrol and guarding the telegraph line, including the men of Company A. However, they considered these activities as voluntary.

"We vol. for home garde, wer not to go out of Maryland, we did however by request of our worthy General Lockwood volunteer for 60 day to go to Virginia as the rebels were gathering in much strength in the Vicinity of Drummingtown, ther was nothing compensory about the matter it was Voluntarily on the part (of) Company A ...."

Private George W. Elliott [xxxv]

"As a matter of fact every company did do duty outside of this territory but it was always considered as a voluntary matter as the character of the organization was never formally changed."

1st Lieut. Thomas H. Coburn [xxxvi]

Not only did they go into Virginia as volunteers, they apparently considered their service as separate from the regular army, more as a local militia organization.

"As fore as Im Capabil of comprehending, caus of Discharge at the time and place was for none Other

perpos than to give them an opertunity to inlist in the reagular army, as many did at that time..."

Private George W. Elliott [xxxvii]

"We guarded the Railroad and telegraph lines, the boys got tired and proposed that (we) would see or write to General Wool who commanded the department and ask for our discharge and go into the 8th Maryland, U.S. Infantry."

Private John H. Ricketts [xxxviii]

The 8th Maryland, U. S. Infantry was organized in Baltimore, Md. in August 1862, about the same time that Company A was about to be discharged. Andrew W. Denison was commissioned Colonel for the regiment. It is likely that the men of Company A had heard of the new regiment mustering in Baltimore. Bothum's account and the local newspaper both relate that after discharge, Capt. J. C. Henry tried to organize a new company, intending to join the 8th Maryland. An article in the Cambridge Herald urged support of Henry's efforts:

"Attention Union Men: What are you doing to suppress this unholy rebellion?....A company is organizing in your midst, to help roll back the tide of war from our beloved state.....do not wait for the draft.... assist Capt. Henry with all the means in your reach, he is worthy of your confidence, a gallant man, whose every pulsation beats for his country's good, in whatever position he may be placed, he will reflect credit on his native county. Arouse then, and come to your country's rescue, in this her time of need."

The Cambridge Herald

From such first-hand accounts, it is apparent that the men of Company A were interested in requesting a discharge in order to 'join the regular army'. Certainly the mundane guard duty assignments might lead many of them to long for the glory of battle, an opportunity to fight for their cause and further their careers as soldiers. Nearly half of the company did re-enlist with other units, some within days of their discharge. Three men joined other companies of the 1st Eastern Shore Regiment. Three others were wounded in battle, including Captain J. C. Henry with the Confederate Army and two were killed in the line of duty, in service in other regiments.

The story of their discharge however becomes tangled in contradiction on the point of who disobeyed an order and what that order was. We know by Sgt. Levin Bothum's account that the company was on a schooner off of Shelltown, Md. near the mouth of the Pocomoke River. Other accounts do not elaborate on this point, neither supporting, nor refuting his statement. Bothum further states that the men stopped at the Maryland / Virginia line and *"would go no fother."* No reason is given, but the wording insinuates a refusal to continue, presumably into Virginia. He relates that Captain J. C. Henry and over a dozen others formed a squad and went into Drummond-town, though the reason for this action is not noted. It was upon the squad's return that the company went back to Newtown and shortly thereafter, received their discharge.

1st Lieut. Thomas Coburn gives his own version of the story: *"In August 1862, Co. A of this Regiment was ordered to proceed to the Eastern Shore of Virginia but when it reached the line between the two states, refused to cross. That is the most of the men so refused, but I, and Lieutenant Mowbray and twenty enlisted men did not refuse, and in fact I and nineteen of the men did proceed to Drummondtown – the point to which the Company was ordered – and did do duty there until ordered by General H. H. Lockwood to rejoin our company."* [xxxix]

The above accounts both confirm the fact that the company had been ordered to report to Drummondtown and boarded a schooner to travel to that location. During their passage down the Pocomoke River, they apparently had second thoughts. Such a disobedience would have been reported to Bridg. General Lockwood by Capt. Henry when the squad reported for duty, minus most of the company. This would certainly give cause for dismissal. The fact that they were not dishonorably discharged might well have been because the order they disobeyed was not a lawful order, in light of their enlistment agreement not to be required to serve beyond the Eastern Shore of Maryland.

However, if over a dozen men, as many as twenty, did indeed do their duty and reported to Drummondtown as ordered, why were the dutiful members discharged with the guilty ones? It should be further noted that Levin Bothum, in spite of his interesting account, was not present at the time. He was not present when the order was given to board the schooner, nor was he aboard the schooner until after the squad had already left for Drummondtown. The original account says *"we liked to get drunk by the time we got there* (the schooner at Shelltown).....*we went aboard the vessel and laid there a week. We had a jolly time of it while there*." While this diminishes the value of Bothum's account, there is still the account of 1st Lieut. Thomas Coburn, who states he was one of those who did their duty. No other account corroborates his story.

Pension records, however, contradict Coburn's statement. Several pension records contain a Pension Appeal dated May 28, 1903, written by A. Parlett Lloyd, of Baltimore, Md. as attorney for John H. Miller, John H. O. Ricketts and others. [xl] Item 3 of the Pension Appeal states *"The Honorable Commissioner (Eugene F. Ware) .... very justly exonerates the men for offenses of their officers...."* Further, Item 7 states: *"Refusal to leave the boundaries of their state was by the officers not by the men themselves..." "Claimant asks allowance of his claim that 1) He faithfully performed his contract of service, 2) He was not responsible for acts of his superior officers...."*

In the words of some of those claimants:

"I clame that my discharge is as honorably ____ as any held today by inlisted soldiers of reblion who lived to get a discharge."

Private George W. Elliott[xli]

"There was nothing in my conduct during my service in Co. A 1st E. S. Md. Vol. Inf. that would call for anything but an honorable discharge."

Private John H. Miller[xlii]

Private Miller elsewhere made oath that he never refused to obey any orders given him by his superior officers and that he was never implicated with any men who did so and he was always ready to do his duty when called upon.

The three highest ranking officers of the company were Captain John C. Henry, 1st Lt. Thomas H. Coburn and 2nd Lt. Clement T. Mowbray. Bothum's account places Capt. Henry in the squad that left the schooner for Drummondtown. The account of Coburn says that he and Mowbray were members of that squad. If the three highest ranking officers of the company were part of the squad that reported to Drummondtown and were the ones who disobeyed orders as accused above, what order did they refuse?

A letter of Lieutenant Adjutant John E. Rastall mentions a bit of information that has been overlooked by other accounts.

(letter home) *August 5, 1862*
Camp Pocahontas (Eastville, Va.)

"I received three papers from you a short time since but letters are very hard. It seems that we are doomed never to be together again. (I mean the companies in this Regt.) for the General has orders to blockade again the entire bay coast even up into Maryland and we have pressed into service dozens of schooners and sloops for the purpose. Every inlett and bay will have a squad of men at its mouth. Three companies of our regiment and a cavalry company are now being posted on the coast...."

Shelltown, Md. is located near the mouth of the Pocomoke River, as it empties into Pocomoke Sound and from there into the Chesapeake Bay.[xliii] Near Shelltown is a convenient vantage point to guard the river, having a good view across the Sound while remaining in the shelter of the banks of the river. Just upriver from Shelltown, the Pocomoke River makes a number of sharp bends, providing opportunity of further shelter from approaching storms. The location offers perfect cover for an ambush or for a defendable line of retreat if such were necessary.

Captain Henry's Company had been stationed the preceding month or so in Newtown, upriver from Shelltown. They would have been the logical choice if a company was needed to guard the river's mouth. Rastall fails to mention which companies were on 'coast guard', nor does a review of military records provide this information. However there are clues. The Regimental Returns of the 1st Eastern Shore Infantry are cards that were filled out monthly to reflect where each company was and what they were doing. Company Muster Roll cards were also filled out for each company every two months. A study of the Regimental Returns and Company Muster Rolls reveals that the cards were filled out at the end of each period and that they give a brief summary of activities. [xliv]

In July we know that the Regimental Field and Staff were in Eastville, Va. Company A was in Newtown, Md. where it had been since June. Company B was stationed at Salisbury, Md., also since June. Where the rest of the companies (8 in all) were for most of July is not noted but July 21, 1862 Companies C, D, E, F, G & K, along with the Field, Staff and Band, left for their 'line of march' in from Eastville to Pungoteague to Franktown and back to Eastville. They were joined in Eastville by Companies H & I and encamped in Camp Pocahontas near Eastville, Va.

The records for August note that Company B was still in Salisbury; Companies C & D left Eastville in late August for Drummondtown; Company E left Eastville late August for Snow Hill; Company F under Capt. Numbers left Eastville August 5th and was stationed at the mouths of different inlets and creeks on the Bayside of the Peninsula extending from Cape Charles to Pungoteague in Accomack County, Va.; Company G left Eastville in late August for Drummondtown; Company H left Eastville in mid-August for Drummondtown; Company I also left Eastville for Drummondtown in late August; Company K was in Princess Anne at some point. The August records for Company A simply note their discharge, with no mention of where they had been earlier in the month.

The movements cited above support Rastall's account that some companies were performing 'coast guard' duty, but only mention one company while Rastall says that there were three companies (in addition to a cavalry unit, unidentified). Not only are the other two 'coast guard' companies not listed, but the records leave a gap in time from late July to late August when they insinuate that most of the companies were in Eastville for nearly a month. However, Jack Rastall says in his letter of August 5th that the companies are *"destined to never to be together again"*. Jack wrote that letter from Eastville and would hardly make that statement if most of the companies were stationed there at the time. One can surmise that the Regimental Records are not exact, but merely a bare outline of their movements. This reveals a window of time in early August when several companies, including Company A, are unaccounted for and might have been on the coast guard duty of which Jack wrote.

If indeed Company A was on coast guard duty in early August, it is very possible that they were posted at the mouth of the Pocomoke River near Shelltown, down river from their previous post. They may have "*stopped and would go no fother"* not because they refused orders, but because this was their assigned post. It would be interesting to read Lt. Adj. Rastall's account of Company A's discharge. Unfortunately he neglected this subject in his letters home. At the time, he was stationed in Camp Pocahontas in Eastville, Va. where he was conducting a court martial. Other excitement at this time was caused by the brief visit of General McClellan to the Eastern Shore of Virginia to use the telegraph. Apparently it was quite the topic of conversation at the time. The only mention Rastall makes of Company A was later in October when he writes from Salisbury *"....we are rapidly filling up to make another Company A....."* It is believed that the second company was never filled.

However, Rastall's failure to comment on the early discharge of Company A may mean that it was not of much concern. Rastall was the clerk and assistant to Colonel Wallace and would surely have heard the news, even if he was not there at the time. His comments on an incident with Company B clearly express his feelings about refusal of orders.

"October 8, 1862 Felton, Del. ....Yesterday afternoon Co. B and I left Salisbury for where no one knew. All the field and staff were on the cars. Co. B is a "home guard" company. It numbered 89 men. We had gone 8 miles on the cars. The horses (field and staff) had been sent ahead and everything seemed quiet and the men cheerful. At the line dividing Del. from Md. there is a little village named Delmar, the first three letters of each state's name combined. Then the train stopped to switch off a freight car. I was sitting with the officers in the rear car when a yell started us and looking out I beheld a sight which brought a blush to my cheeks. Co.B had revolted and were throwing everything they had out of the cars and their effects head over heels. 89 men went out – 10 returned. They stacked arms, took off everything belonging to U. Sam except clothing which they got from government and lay down. Here was a __ in earnest. I calculated in an instant – Here were 79 men, all sober to a man and firm.

In the cars were 52 men of Co. I, a Baltimore company half of which were drunk. They kept their seats. Some of them the floor. The Colonel turned white. I turned red. What was to be done. Here we are sent on important Government business with 2 car loads of arms, ammunition and luggage. The Col. ordered them to equip themselves and march east to Salisbury. This they refused to do. We then tumbled all their things aboard and left them in the woods sitting on the canteens of their knapsacks.... A company from below is sent up to ___ and I hope they will succeed in catching every one of them. I never want to see that sight again."[xlv]

From Rastall's strong disapproval of the above described revolt, one might wonder why he did not comment on the early discharge of Company A if it was the result of such disobedience. At the very least he might be expected to comment on the discharge when he wrote of filling a new company.

A copy of a letter written by Capt. Henry's daughter Willie many years after the War states that her father's company disbanded because most of the boys were of "southern proclivities".[xlvi] Considering her father's later service in the Confederacy, this opinion might be understandable. However, 28% of Company A re-enlisted in the Union Army, 10% enlisted as draftees and served in the Union Army and 7% went back into Union service as paid substitutes after the draft, resulting in nearly half of the company supporting the Union in active regiments away from home. Many of these men went back into service shortly after their discharge. These statistics do not support the idea that most of them were of southern proclivities, nor do they describe a group of men who did not want to leave home in service of their country.

There was one other incident on the Shore concerning refusal to obey orders. February 1863 Brigadier General Lockwood's Brigade was ordered to Baltimore, and was shortly thereafter sent to Gettysburg. The majority of Company K, of the 1st E. S. Maryland. Volunteers refused to leave the Shore. It was their contention that they enlisted as Home Guard under the agreement that they would not be ordered away from their home area. The advertisement in the Cambridge Herald and elsewhere specifically stated that they would be stationed on the Eastern Shore of Maryland. The result of Company K's refusal to leave the Delmarva Peninsula led to the dishonorable discharge of those involved. The remainder of the company continued on with the brigade.

The assurance of remaining in their home area surely led to discipline problems. Company B's revolt led to the entire company's arrest and disciplinary action (minus the 10 who returned to the train). Company K's refusal to leave the Delmarva Peninsula got them a dishonorable discharge. For Company A, their discharge is more vague. The Cambridge Herald says they disbanded. The military record of each soldier in Company A bears a typed note that says: *"The word 'honorably' in certificate of muster-out roll is erased."*

More official documentation is not as specific as one would like. A document dated December 28, 1895 from G. Norman Lieber, Judge Advocate General was furnished to the Commissioner of Pensions March 29, 1900. It acknowledges that the Regiment was accepted by the Secretary of War as a Home Guard in a letter addressed to Col. James Wallace August 16, 1861. It also references a letter from the War Department to Governor Hicks on September 4, 1861 in which it states that the *"regiment from the Eastern Shore is accepted as a State Guard except in case of special necessity."* The newspaper advertisement in the Cambridge Herald stating the terms of enlistment is also sited. The document further quotes a report from Brig. General Lockwood to Corps Headquarters on August 5, 1862 in which Lockwood states that *"Co. A refused to cross the line into Virginia when ordered so to do and asks for instructions."* The instructions from Headquarters was quoted as stating *"Lockwood will muster out of service the company that refused to cross over the line to*

Drummondtown, Va., stating the reason on the muster out roll." This informative document goes on to quote the Letters Received Book of the Middle Dept. *"August 8, 1862... relative to the refusal of 60 men of the 1st Eastern Shore Vols. to cross the line into Virginia – records do not show whether any action was taken on this paper, nor has the paper been found on the files."*

Pension Commission records state that the Company was discharged without honor and the document of Judge Advocate General Lieber claims that the Certificate of Mustering Officer says *"word honorably in certificate was evidently lined out by the mustering officer"*. However, a scanned copy of the Certificate is found online in which the word honorable is most definitely not lined out and statements from several members of the company indicate that they were unaware of the 'Discharge Without Honor'. A copy of the Certificate is included above. The Order of Major General Wool of August 12, 1862 *"has not been found of record"*. The conflicting evidence continues to cloud the picture of what happened off Shelltown, Md. in early August 1862.

By all accounts, Company A was ordered to Drummondtown, Va. and was mustered out of service for the disobedience that order. Their discharge appears to have originally been 'With Honor' but was changed to 'Without Honor' many years later by the Pension Commission. Conflicting accounts present two scenarios. 1) The Company was ordered to Drummondtown by boat via the Pocomoke River. The enlisted men stopped the schooner from crossing into Virginia and the top three officers, along with nearly twenty enlisted men, marched to Drummondtown as ordered, but were discharged along with the rest of the Company. Or 2) The Company was posted at Shelltown as coast guard. Some of the men had talked of asking for a discharge so that they could re-enlist with the 'regular army', apparently the 8th Maryland. The three top officers, along with nearly twenty enlisted men, formed a squad to march to Drummondtown, Va. to seek said discharge. If the result of the squad's meeting with Lockwood involved a disobedience and subsequent discharge, perhaps Lockwood ordered the Company back to Drummondtown and the officers refused. It would be possible that the majority of the men back on the schooner never knew of the order or the refusal, knew only that they had been granted the discharge they had anticipated.

Private Bothum relates in his memoirs that after the discharge, there was a misunderstanding between Capt. Henry and Colonel Andrew W. Denison, of the 8th Maryland; his plans for a new company had failed. No mention is made of the nature of their disagreement. Captain Henry was obviously determined to raise another company, as The Cambridge Herald months later encouraged readers to join Capt. Henry. However, an Order had recently been issued that might have interfered with Henry's plans. General Order, No. 99 of the War Dept., Washington, August 9, 1862 laid out regulations for the upcoming draft and enrollment of 300,000 militia. The seventh and final article of that order stated: *"From and after the 15th day of August no new regiments of volunteers will be organized, but the premium, bounty and advance pay will continue to be paid to those volunteering to go into the old regiments."* [xlvii] This meant that should Captain Henry succeed in gathering enough men for a company, they would not serve together, but be split up and assigned to fill existing companies. No new companies could be formed until the draft was complete and all vacancies were filled. If it was Henry's intention to disband Company A in order to enlist his men as a company with the 8th Maryland, he was too late.

In November Dorchester County held a draft to meet their portion of the state's quota. J. C. Henry was among the men drafted into service. It was the practice during the Civil War that a draftee could pay a fee to be released from service, or hire a substitute. J. C. Henry hired a substitute named John H. Shaw of Washington to take his place in the draft. It seems that he wished to serve on his own terms. Months later, still unable to organize a new company for the Union, he left for Richmond and enlisted with the 2nd Maryland of the Confederate Army. It has been suggested that he took some local men with him, supposedly from the 1st Eastern Shore Regiment, but this has yet to be confirmed.

Likely we will never know what happened on the schooner off of Shelltown, or what transpired when Captain Henry and his associates went to Drummondtown. It is the opinion of this writer that Captain John C. Henry refused orders to free himself and his men from service in order to organize a new unit for the 8th Maryland, thereby furthering his own military career. Unfortunately for him, the company was disbanded too late for him to have his own company with the 8th Maryland, and rather than be assigned randomly in a Union company, he elected to join the Confederacy. Some of his men re-enlisted with other units within weeks and more re-enlisted that Fall. A few took advantage of the draft by hiring themselves out as substitutes. Nearly half of the company re-joined the Union Army and bravely served in active duty out of the state Maryland, where two were wounded and two more were killed in action.

Chicago, Dec. 8, 1902.

Hon. Chas. F. Scott,
House of Representatives,
Washington, D.C.

My dear Sir:

.....Now Mr. Scott, that whole company (Co. A, 1st Eastern Shore Maryland Volunteers) should be restored, except those who went south and joined the confederacy. I sincerely wish I might be summoned before the Pension committee of the House to tell the story of that regiment which story is a long one and most novel and interesting. I was adjutant of it for three years, and did much of the mustering-in of both officers and men. I wish J. H. Ricketts could get a pension. I believe he deserves it as much as any old soldier in your district, but he is barred because he did not re-enlist after muster-out "without honor". The Captain of his company, John C. Henry, went south and fought in the confederate service,together with all the men he could induce to follow him. Our regiment (his) fought the confederate regiment at Gettysburg, face to face, to which he was attached, and we captured one of our old comrades wounded, whom we had mustered out "without honor". Our Chaplain as soon as he heard of the presence of our old comrades of Co. A in our front, through this wounded rebel, loaded himself with canteens, and deliberately went to attend their wounded. They captured the Chaplain, stole his horse and his personal belongings, and turned him loose and he came back into our lines. This at base of Culp's Hill.

Very respectfully,

John E. Rastall

P.S. This in reply to your letter of Dec. 6, 1902.[xlviii]

APPENDIX- A

SHELLTOWN SQUAD

The squad from Company A, 1st E. S. Regt. that left the schooner near Shelltown, Md. for Drummondtown, Va. was made up of nearly twenty men. Captain John C. Henry, 1st Lieut. Thomas H. Coburn and 2nd Lieut. Clement T. Mowbray were reportedly a part of this squad. No other details have been found about this pivotal event that led to the company's early discharge. The names of the rest of the members of the squad may never be known for certain. A careful review of military records indicate that most of Company A were mustered out at Newtown, Md., including 1st Lieut. Coburn and 2nd Lieut. Mowbray. Capt. Henry was mustered out in Eastville, Va., perhaps due to his rank as Captain. However, a number of men were mustered out in Drummondtown, Va.. This group, coincidentally or not, numbers fifteen, just the right number of men to make up the squad from Shelltown.

Shelltown Squad *Confirmed*

Capt. John C. Henry

1st Lieut. Thomas H. Coburn

2nd Lieut. Clement T. Mowbray

Tentative List

*re-enlisted Union regiment

Charles S. Blades	William Jones	James W. Straughn
James H. Cooper*	Noah F. Lewis*	Joseph W. Warren
Levin W. Dail*	Lewis W. Merrick*	Charles H. Way*
Joseph H.Hodson	Thomas W.A.Stevens	Thomas H.Wherrett*
Jenkins Horseman*	Charles E. Stewart	

Absent from the Schooner

William B. Sweed, *died of pneumonia winter 1861-2*

Patrick Henrettie, *committed to asylum in Washington, D.C. early summer 1862*

Wilber F. Newton, *transferred to Regiment, Non-commissioned officer*

William T. Robinson, *transferred to Regiment as Non-commissioned officer*

Charles R. Blades, *transferred to Regimental Band*

W. Dallas Lednum, *transferred to Regimental Band*

Walter M. Kirby, *on detached service, Philadelphia July 1862, possibly absent from schooner?*

Hugh C. Bennett, *Spring 1862 in Drummondtown, Va. awaiting sentence, charges unknown.*

John S. Cornwell, *Spring 1862 in Drummondtown, Va. awaiting sentence, charges unknown.*

Josiah F. Robinson, *deserted May 24, 1862*

Robert A. Conaway, *deserted August 1, 1862*

Aaron G. Cook, *deserted August 1, 1862*

Joseph M. Smith, *deserted August 1, 1862*

APPENDIX- B

ROLL CALL

Henry, John Campbell Captain

John C. Henry was born 1840 in East New Market, Md. to Francis Jenkins Henry & Wilhelmina Goldsborough Henry. His father was clerk of court in Cambridge and in 1860 J. C. was working as a store clerk. September 11, 1861 he enlisted with the 1st E. S. Md. Vols. in Cambridge. He was instrumental in the enlistment and organization of Company A. August 16, 1862 he mustered out in Eastville, Va.

After his discharge J. C. returned to Cambridge and attempted to enlist a new company for the 8th Md., but was not successful due to a disagreement with the Colonel of the 8th Md. He continued his efforts to organize a new company, in spite of being drafted in the Dorchester County draft. He hired a substitute, John H. Shaw of Washington to take his place. His efforts were noted in the Cambridge Herald, encouraging local young men to join him in his efforts.

Apparently the response was disappointing. Many of J. C.'s men from the disbanded Company A had re-enlisted elsewhere. January 1862 J. C. secretly left for Richmond, Va. where he enlisted with Company A of the 2nd Md., C. S. He was mustered in March 19, 1862 in Richmond by Capt. R. B. Winder, likely a relative. A letter written to his mother the following year indicates that he did not tell even his family he was leaving, as his parents were supporters of the Union.

Henry was at Culp's Hill during the 3rd day of the Battle of Gettysburg, where he fought against members of the 1st Eastern Shore Volunteers, men he had served with during his time in the Union Army. August 16, 1864 J. C. was wounded at Weldon Railroad, Va. and spent time as a patient in Robertson Hospital in Richmond. He is listed on the Register of Prisoners April 1865, was was paroled in Farmville, Va. by T. L. Barker, Lieut. Col. of the 36th Massachusetts Vols. His Oath of Allegiance was administered by Colonel Woolley May 16, 1865.

After the War, J. C. returned to Cambridge, where he married Ann E. Lake, with whom he had several children. He worked as a store clerk. In the late 1800's J. C. and Ann moved to New Orleans, Louisiana with at least some of their family. J. C. died circa 1900 in New Orleans.

Coburn, Thomas H. 1st Lieutenant

Thomas H. Coburn was born January 2, 1830. In 1850 he was living in Dorchester County in a boarding house run by Benton Crocket and was working as a bricklayer. By 1860 he was in Cambridge with an apprentice of his own, living with his wife Adelia and their family.

Thomas enlisted with the 1st E. S. September 11, 1861 in Cambridge where he was elected 1st Lieutenant on the boat from Potters Landing. In June 1862 he was absent from his company on detached service in Washington D.C., taking Private Patrick Henrettie to the asylum. He accompanied Capt. Henry to Drummondtown that summer of 1862, just before the company was discharged. He mustered out August 16, 1862 at Newtown. He was living in Easton, Md. in 1890 and filed for pension in 1891. He died March 2, 1901 and is buried in Spring Hill Cemetery, Easton, Md.

Mowbray, Clement, T. 2nd Lieutenant

Clement T. Mowbray was born 1835, the son of James F. and Eliza A. Mowbray. The family was living in Dorchester County, 1st District in 1850. March 7, 1861 Clement married Sarah Rebecca Reese in Dorchester County. He was 5' 11 ¾" tall, with hazel eyes and black hair. He made a living as a shoemaker. September 11, 1861 he enlisted with the 1st E. S. Vols. in Cambridge. According to Thomas Coburn's affidavit in his pension record, Clement was part of the squad that left the boat near Shelltown for Drummondtown. He mustered out August 16, 1862 in Newtown.

During the Dorchester County draft of 1862, Clement was drafted. It is unknown if he served, or was released. His widow Sarah filed for pension in 1907.

Adkins, Levin Private

Levin Adkins was born about 1820 to Samuel and Leah Harvey Adkins of East New Market, Dorchester County, Md.. Levin married Sally Ann Hayes October 1, 1845. According to the 1850 Dorchester County Census, Levin worked as a laborer. Sally Ann died in 1848 leaving Levin with two young children, John & Mary Ann. In about 1855 Levin married Sarah Ann Colbourne, with whom he had nine children.

When the Civil War began, Levin was about 41 years of age and raising four children with Sarah. He had hazel eyes and auburn hair and was working as a farmer. He enlisted with J. C. Henry on October 12, 1861 in Cambridge, was transferred briefly to Stafford's Company E and then transferred back to Henry's Company, Company A. Levin was severely handicapped by rheumatism, complicated by his service in the 1st Eastern Shore Md. Vols. which required him to sleep in all kinds of weather and locations. Levin was mustered out of service August 16, 1862 at Newtown, Md.

After the war Levin returned to farming, living in the Vienna District of Dorchester County. He received a pension in 1889. Levin died circa 1899-1900, survived by his wife Sarah, who died 1913.

Airey, Andrew Private

Andrew Airey was born between 1820-25. At the start of the War Andrew was living in Cambridge with his wife Elizabeth and their four children, while working as a fisherman. He enlisted with the 1st E. S. Md. Vols. September 11, 1861 in Cambridge. He mustered out in Newtown August 16, 1862 and returned to his growing family in Cambridge. He received a pension in 1890.

Alexander, William J. Private

William J. Alexander was born 1836 and enlisted in the 1st E. S. Md. Vols. September 11, 1861 in Cambridge. He mustered out in Newtown August 16, 1862 and re-enlisted in

Newtown less than two weeks later, this time as Private in Company A of Purnell's Legion, Cavalry. He furnished his own horse and equipment. He was likely with Purnell's Legion during the Battle of Gettysburg. February 1865 he was absent from his company, detached at Eastville, Va assigned to the Quarter Master Department. William was discharged and mustered out June 2, 1865 at Fortress Monroe, Va.

Anthony, John / Jonathon H. Private

John Anthony was born 1821 in Carlisle, Pa. At the time of his enlistment, he was 5' 8" with a dark complexion, black eyes and black hair. He was employed as a hemp maker. John enlisted September 11, 1861 in Cambridge with J. C. Henry. He was absent briefly in November of the same year, out sick. August 16, 1862 he mustered out in Newtown. Nearly a year later, July 7, 1863, John re-enlisted in Baltimore for six months with Company G, 10th Md. Infantry as a Private. He was promoted shortly after to Company Corporal. John mustered out January 29, 1864. He received a pension in 1879 and is listed on the 1883 List of Pensioners of Cambridge.

Applegarth, George H. Private

George H. Applegarth was born 1839 to George and Mary Hubbard Applegarth of Dorchester County, Md. At the time of the War George worked on the water as a mariner and lived in the 8th District of Dorchester County. He enlisted in 1st E. S. Md. Vols. September 11, 1861 in Cambridge and mustered out in Newtown August 16, 1862. After the War he lived in Cornersville, Dorchester County near his parents, making his living as a farmer.

Bamburger, Joseph H. Private

Joseph H. Bamburger was born in December 1840 in Cambridge, though he may have lived in Baltimore City for a time before the War and worked as a bricklayer. He was listed as a farmer at the time of enlistment and later as a sailor. September

11, 1861 Joseph enlisted with the 1st E. S. Md. Vols. in Cambridge with J. C. Henry and mustered out August 16, 1862 in Newtown. Nearly two years later Joseph re-enlisted on July 9, 1864 in Baltimore for one hundred days as a Private with Company C, 12th Md. Joseph stood 5' 4" with a light complexion, blue eyes and light hair. In 1900 he was still working on the water as a sailor in Cambridge, at the age of fifty nine. He filed for a pension in 1891 and died in 1927.

Bell, Levin Private

Levin Bell was born 1838, the son of Jacob and Rhoda Ellingsworth Bell of Dorchester ("Dorset") County, Md. Levin married Margaret J. Valliant August 18, 1850 and was employed as a laborer and farmer in Cambridge shortly before the War. Levin stood 5' 5 ½" with a dark complexion, grey/hazel eyes and black hair. He enlisted September 21, 1861 in Cambridge with J. C. Henry, 1st E. S. Md. Vols. and mustered out August 16, 1862 in Newtown. Within three months Levin was drafted in the Dorchester County draft and sent to Camp Hicks (aka Camp Kirby) in Easton. He is listed as having a deformed middle finger in the right hand.

Levin was enrolled February 13, 1863 in Baltimore for nine months as a Private with Company B, 5th Md. April 7, 1863 he was absent from duty, sick in the post hospital at Harpers Ferry, Va. He mustered out December 9, 1863 in Baltimore and returned to Dorchester County, living in Vienna with his wife Margaret and their children. Levin filed for a pension in 1886.

Bennett, Hugh C. Private

Hugh C. Bennett was born in "Dorset County" (Dorchester) Md. in 1816. He lived in Cornersville before the War. Hugh was 5' 10 ½" tall, with a dark complexion, hazel eyes and brown hair and was likely the oldest soldier in Company A, being about forty five years old. He was a carpenter by trade. He enlisted in the 1st E. S. Md. Vols. September 11, 1862 with Clement Mowbray in Cambridge. He was arrested March 1862 and held in Drummondtown awaiting sentence of court martial.

The result of his court martial is unknown, as he was mustered out with the rest of his company August 16, 1862 in Newtown, Md.

Hugh returned to Cornersville after his discharge where he lived with his wife Sarah Elizabeth and their several children. He was deceased by June 1890, when his widow filed for pension.

Blades, Charles R. Private

Charles R. Blades was born in Talbot County, Md. in 1841, the son of Samuel H. and Elizabeth Blades. The family lived in St. Michaels where his father worked on the water as a sailor. Charles had hazel eyes and dark hair. He enlisted September 24, 1861 in the 1st E. S. Md. Vols. in St. Michaels. Apparently Charles had a talent for music, as he transferred to the Regiment's Band November 1, 1861. After serving his three year term, he re-enlisted in Baltimore for one year with Company H, 1st E. S. Md. and was again detached from his company to the Regimental Band. He was transferred with the rest of the 1st E. S. to the 11th Md. Infantry in the latter part of the War and remained with the Band. He mustered out for the final time in Baltimore June 15, 1865.

Charles is said to be buried in the Olivet Cemetery behind St. Luke's United Methodist Church in St. Michaels, though his grave is unmarked. His death was a suicide.

Blades, Charles S. Private

Charles S. Blades was born in Talbot County, Md. April 1840 to Thomas and Mary A. Blades. His father was a ship's carpenter and Charles followed in his father's footsteps, studying as an apprentice to Master Carpenter Jeremiah Muris of Easton. Carpentry may not have agreed with him, as he listed himself as a sailor at the time of his enlistment. Charles stood 5' 8 ½" , with a light complexion, blue eyes and light hair. He enlisted September 24, 1861 in St. Michaels with J. C. Henry, 1st E. S. Md. Vols. He mustered out August 16, 1862 in Drummondtown, Va. Years after the War he was employed as a teamster in St. Michaels, living with his wife Elizabeth and their family. He filed for pension in 1890 and died January 14, 1907.

Bothum, Levin W. Sergeant

Levin W. Bothum was born about 1840 in New Jersey, the son of Levin Dashiell Bothum and Elinor B. Langsdale Bothum. The family had moved to Cambridge, Md. when Levin was very young. At the time of his enlistment, Levin was 5' 10" with a dark complexion, dark hazel eyes and dark hair and was employed as a blacksmith. He enlisted in the 1st E. S. Md. Vols. September 11, 1861 with J. C. Henry in Cambridge. He was voted Sergeant when the Company chose their officers on the boat returning to Cambridge from Potter's Landing. October 1861 Levin was on duty repairing guns. It is Levin's memoirs that have been quoted earlier, providing details of the service of Company A. He was on leave when Company A boarded the schooner just prior to their discharge. He joined the company at the boat near Shelltown along with Harrison Winterbottom and Levin Dail. Bothum mustered out at Newtown August 16, 1862.

He re-enlisted two months later September 30, 1862 in Baltimore as a Private with Company G, 8th Md. Infantry. He was promoted to Orderly Sergeant the following week. During his service with the 8th Md., Levin was wounded July 18, 1864 near Petersburg, Va by a sniper shot in the stomach. He spent time recovering in DeCamp Hospital, David's Island in New York Harbor and then to Jarvis U. S. A. General Hospital in Baltimore. He returned to duty April 19, 1865.

After the War Levin married Annie Mamie Kirby, the daughter of Major George W. Kirby of Camp Kirby in Easton, Md. It appears that Annie died before 1880. Levin lived with his widowed mother and his son Herman and worked as a tin merchant. Levin's memoir was written years after the War in the back pages of Major Kirby's Camp Ledger. He filed for pension 1892. He died August 13, 1917 in Cambridge where he is buried. His mother out lived him and collected on his pension in 1917.

Bradshaw, William E. S. Private

William E. S. Bradshaw was born 1842, probably in Dorchester County, Md. Census records indicate that he may have been the son of Tyler Bradshaw of Hart's Store area, 10th District. September 11, 1861 William enlisted with the 1st E. S. Vols. in East New Market and mustered out August 16, 1862 in Newtown. A William Bradshaw was drafted months later in the Somerset County draft, likely the same who had been so recently discharged. William chose to hire a substitute, John White from Scotland.

Bromwell, William Private

William Bromwell was born 1837. He may have been the son of Thomas Bromwell, a farmer in Talbot County. In 1860 he was living in Bay Hundred District, Talbot County, working as a farmer. He enlisted in the 1st E. S. Vols. September 24, 1861 in St. Michaels and mustered out August 16, 1862 in Newtown.

Burk, James M. Private

James M. Burk was from Philadelphia, Pa., born 1841. He was 5' 5" with a light complexion, grey eyes and dark hair. When the war began he was making his living as a farmer. James enlisted September 11, 1861 in the 1st Eastern Shore Vols. with J. C. Henry in East New Market and mustered out August 16, 1862 in Newtown.

Cantwell, Joseph H. Private

Joseph H. Cantwell was born 1840 in "Dorset" or Dorchester County, Md. He may have been the son of Thomas and Amelia Mowbray Cantwell. In 1850 Milly (nickname for Amelia?) was widowed with a son Josiah named among her children.

Regardless, Joseph of Company A stood 5' 10 ½" tall with a light complexion, blue eyes and light hair. He was a sailor until he enlisted in the 1st E. S. Md. Vols. September 11,1861 with

J. C. Henry in Cambridge. He mustered out August 16, 1862 in Newtown. One month later, September 19 Joseph re-enlisted with Theodore Clayton in Company C, Purnell's Legion, Cavalry in Baltimore. He deserted temporarily in January 1863 and was present with his company again in the Spring. Joseph was killed in action at Petersburg, Va. July 7, 1864, one of two from the original Company A to be killed in action.

Chance, Robert A Private

Robert A. Chance was from Caroline County, born 1841. He stood 5' 5 ½", dark complexion with dark hazel eyes and dark hair. Before the war he had been employed as a clerk. He enlisted with the 1st E. S. Md. September 24, 1861 in St. Michaels and mustered out August 16, 1862 in Newtown. Shortly thereafter he enlisted with Company C, Purnell's Legion, Cavalry, recruited by Theodore Layton in Baltimore. Robert spent the Spring 1863 detached from his company on special service in Baltimore. He spent the late summer that year in Satteries U.S.A. General Hospital, West Philadelphia with chronic rheumatism. His company transferred to the 8th Md., Company I. He remained missing from his company due to illness into the Spring of 1865, being mustered out May 31 the same year at Arlington Heights.

After the War, Robert went back to work as a clerk in Centreville, Md. He later moved back to Caroline County where he lived with his wife Josephine and family.

Conaway, Robert A. Private

Robert A. Conaway was born 1838 in Caroline County, Md. He was the son of Dr. John W. and Ann M. Conaway. Robert was 5' 6" tall with dark complexion, grey eyes, dark hair & worked as a carpenter. He enlisted in the 1st E. S. September 16, 1861 in Federalsburg. He transferred briefly to Capt. Stafford's Company E and then back to Company A with Capt. Henry. Robert deserted August 1, 1862, less than two weeks before the rest of the company was discharged. Two others deserted the same day.

Robert re-enlisted September 5, 1862 with E. G. Goldsborough near Hagerstown, Md. with the 8th Md., Company E. He was promoted to Sergeant December 1, 1862 and to Sergeant Stretcher Corps. July 1863. In early 1864, his family wrote to his superiors in an effort to get leave for Robert to visit home, as his father was dangerously ill. It is unknown if he was able to visit his father at that time, or if his father recovered from his illness. Robert was absent from his company in November 1864 on detached duty and on furlough in the Spring of 1865. He mustered out at Arlington Heights, Va. May 30, 1865. He filed for pension in 1890 and was living in Cambridge.

Cook, Aaron G. Private

Aaron G. Cook was born in the late 1820's in Dorchester County, Md. He may have married Nancy J. Tall in 1856, but if so she died not long after, as she is not listed with Aaron in any census records. Aaron stood 5' 9 ½" with a dark complexion, brown eyes and dark hair. He was a mariner and ship's carpenter. Aaron enlisted in the 1st E. S. Md. Vols. September 11, 1861 with J. C. Henry in Cambridge and deserted August 1, 1862, one of three to desert less than two weeks before the entire company was discharged.

Aaron re-enlisted the following month in Baltimore with the 4th Md., Company D, where he was promoted to Sergeant February 12, 1864. He mustered out May 31, 1865 at Arlington Heights, Va. After the War he continued his trade as ship's carpenter in Tobacco Stick, Dorchester County.

Cook, Babylon A. Private

Babylon A. Cook was born in Dorchester County 1826. He was 5' 8 ½" tall, with a dark complexion, grey eyes and dark hair. He was a sailor. He enlisted September 17, 1861 in the 1st E. S. with J. C. Henry in Cambridge. That October he was absent on detached service to guard the steamer Balloon en route to Salisbury, Md. He was mustered out August 16, 1862 in Newtown. He filed for pension in 1871.

Cooper, James H. Private

James H. Cooper was born in Talbot County about 1841/2. His father was deceased by 1850, survived by James's mother Dorothy and sister Ellen, who married Daniel Lednum. James and his sister Ellen's family lived together or near each other for years. James stood 5' 9" tall with a light complexion, blue eyes and dark hair. He made his living as a farmer.

James enlisted in the 1st E. S. with J. W. Straugh in St. Michaels October 2, 1861 and was mustered out August 16, 1862 in Drummondtown, Va. He was drafted shortly thereafter in the Talbot County draft. He re-enlisted in the 9th Md., Company B where he sometimes used the name James H. Jackson. In January 1864 he was on duty as company cook. He mustered out February 23, 1864 in Baltimore.

After the War, James returned to Talbot County, where he lived with his wife Sarah E and their son William and daughter Mary. He made his living as an oysterman. Sarah apparently died in the 1870's and James moved in with his sister Ellen Lednum and her family. He filed for pension in 1890 and died April 24, 1925 in Tilghman, Md.

Cornwell, John S. Private

John S. Cornwell, son of William Cornwell, was born 1820 in St. George's Parish, Accomack County, Va. He later moved to Dorchester County, Md. where he married Mary A. Harper September 13, 1848. He stood 5' 7", with a light complexion, grey eyes and dark hair. He was a tailor by trade. At the age of 41, John enlisted in the 1st E. S. Md. Vols. with J. C. Henry in East New Market on September 11, 1861. He was absent from his company in May 1862 awaiting sentence of court martial in Drummondtown, Va. The result of his court martial is unknown. He mustered out August 16, 1862. John enlisted later with the 8th Md., Company E.

After the War John lived with his wife Mary, their four children and his mother in law Eliza Harper in Vienna, Md. John was a keeper of the Hooper Strait Lighthouse. The first lighthouse at the Straits was torn loose by ice and carried down the Bay in the winter of 1877. John and his assistant barely escaped on one of the light's boats and were trapped on the ice for 24 hours before being rescued. The lighthouse was located some five miles down the Bay and the lens, lamp & fog bell were salvaged. Another lighthouse was built in its place in 1879 and John Cornwell was its first keeper. This lighthouse is stands today at the Chesapeake Bay Maritime Museum in St. Michaels, Md. John filed for pension in 1886.

Cummings, Charles W. P. Private

Charles W. P. Cummings was born 1840, probably in Talbot County, Md. He was the son of Larrimore and Margaret Cummings. Charles and his brother John (below) both enlisted with the 1st E. S. Vols. September 24, 1861 in St. Michaels. They both mustered out August 16, 1862 in Newtown. Charles' widow filed for pension July 1890.

Cummings, John W. K. Private

John W. K. Cummings was born 1843, the son of Larrimore and Margaret Cummings of Talbot County. John and his brother Charles (above) both enlisted with the 1st E. S. Vols. September 24, 1861 in St. Michaels. They both mustered out August 16, 1862 in Newtown.

John was drafted in the Talbot County draft Fall 1862. He was 5' 9 ½" tall, with grey eyes and dark hair. He was a farm hand, following in his father's footsteps. John enlisted with the 9th Md., Company B in Baltimore June 20, 1863 and mustered out February 23, 1864 in Baltimore.

After the War John lived in Tilghman, Md. and filed for pension in 1907. He died May 19, 1910.

Dail, George W. Private

George W. Dail was born 1839. In 1850 George was living with a brother (?) Levin and Elizabeth Dail (mother?) and (relative?) Nathan Ward, a carpenter. When the War began, George was living in the household of William Lee in the

Cambridge area, working as a carpenter. September 19, 1861 George enlisted in the 1st E. Shore in Cambridge. His brother Levin W. Dail had enlisted in the same unit the week before. George mustered out August 16, 1862 in Newtown. After the War, he continued to work as a carpenter in the Cambridge area.

Dail, Levin A. Sergeant

Levin A. Dail was born 1840, the son of William B. Dail of Dorchester County, Md. At the start of the War he made his living as a mariner out of Cambridge and farmed. Levin was 5' 5" with a light complexion, blue eyes and light hair. On September 11, 1861 he enlisted with the 1st E. S. Md. Vols. with J. C. Henry in Cambridge. He mustered out August 16, 1682 in Newtown. After the War he lived in his brother Samuel's home with their sisters Emma and Ida. He filed for pension in 1891.

Dail, Levin W. Private

Levin W. Dail was born in Dorchester County 1843. He enlisted September 11, 1861 in the 1st E. S., signing up with J. C. Henry in Cambridge. His brother George enlisted the following week. Levin was absent from his company October 1861 while on detached service to guard the steamer Balloon on its way to Salisbury, Md. Levin mustered out August 16, 1862 in Drummondtown, Va.

After the draft of Dorchester County Fall 1862, Levin re-enlisted as a substitute for Thomas J. Dail (below, relation?). Levin was described as 5' 8" with hazel eyes and dark brown hair. He worked as a farmer. He was assigned to Company C of the 1st E. S. Vols. He was with the 1st Eastern Shore when they defended Culp's Hill during the Battle of Gettysburg July 3, 1863. He transferred November 17, 1864 to the 3rd Md., Company F and later transferred again to the 11th Md. Company E, where he mustered out June 15, 1865 in Baltimore.

After the War Levin worked in Cambridge as an oysterman and married Ann Eliza Thomas. They lived in Cambridge and had four children. He filed for pension in 1890, and died July 5, 1924.

Dail, Thomas J. Private

Thomas J. Dail was the son of Joseph and Betsy Dail, born 1843 in Dorchester County, Md. He enlisted September 11, 1861 in Cambridge with the 1st E. S., with the consent of his mother due to his young age. He mustered out August 16, 1862 in Newtown. Months later he was drafted in Dorchester County and hired a substitute, Levin W. Dail (above). Thomas enlisted September 30, 1862 in Baltimore with the 8th Md., Company G and mustered out May 31, 1865 in Arlington Heights, Va.

Danielly (Dannelly, Daniels), Henry, E. Private

Henry E. Danielly was born in Philadelphia, Pa. in 1837. He enlisted in the 1st E. S. Md. Vols. with J. C. Henry September 24, 1861 in St. Michaels. He was 5' 5" tall, with a light complexion, grey eyes and light hair. He made his living as a sailor. He mustered out August 16, 1862 in Newtown.

Henry re-enlisted August 30, 1862 in Purnells Legion, Cavalry Company C. He was recruited by Theodore Clayton in Baltimore. In October of the same year, Henry was promoted to Corporal. On January 18, 1864 he was reduced to Private for disobedience of orders. February 14, 1865 he transferred to the 8th Md.., Company I. Henry returned to Easton, Md. after the War, where he worked as a farm laborer. He filed for pension in 1890.

Davis, George M. Private

George M. Davis was born in New York City, NY. 1842. He enlisted in the 1st E. S. Vols. September 11, 1861 in St. Michaels with the written consent of his mother, due to his young age. He mustered out August 16, 1862 in Newtown. That Fall, after the draft of Talbot County, he hired out as a substitute for A. Levi. He re-enlisted with the 3rd Md., Company F February 21, 1863 with Major Wharton in Baltimore for nine months. April 17, 1863 he was employed as nurse at St. Aloysius U. S. A. General Hospital, in Washington, D.C. May 1863 he was absent from his company due to illness. He was in the hospital thru

June. He was mustered out August 20, 1863 by Major Wharton in Baltimore, having fulfilled his nine month obligation.

Edgell, Levi S. Private

Levi S. Edgell was born June 1836 in Caroline County, Md. to Thomas A. and Rhoda Covey Edgell. On October 2, 1861, Levi enlisted with the 1st E. S. Vols. with J. W. Straughn in St. Michaels. He stood 5' 7" and had a light complexion, blue eyes and light hair. He worked as a farmer. He mustered out August 16, 1862 in Newtown.

Levi married Mary C. Neal in 1865 and later married Sarah Emma Nelson in 1870. Levi and Sarah lived in the Trappe District of Talbot County and later moved to Easton, Md. Levi filed for pension in 1890. He died in 1923.

Elliott, George W. Private

George W. Elliott was born August 25, 1838 in Laurel, Delaware. Before the War, George lived in Vienna, Dorchester County, Md. and was employed as a wheelwright. He stood 5' 6" tall and had a dark complexion, grey eyes and dark hair. September 11, 1861 he enlisted with the 1st E. S. in Vienna. He mustered out August 16, 1861 in Newtown.

George married Mary A. Webster January 12, 1864 in Dorchester County. They had no children. He filed for pension in 1890 and died October 3, 1906 in East New Market, Md., where he is buried.

Fairbank, Joshua M. Private

Joshua M. Fairbank, son of Josiah of St. Michaels District, Talbot County, Md. was born March 17, 1838. September 24, 1861 Joshua enlisted with the 1st E. S. with J. C. Henry in St. Michaels. He was about 5' 6" tall, with a dark complexion, hazel eyes and dark hair. At the time of the War, he was working as a sailor and farmer. He mustered out August 16, 1862 in Newtown.

In the Talbot County Draft, Fall of 1862, Joshua hired out as a substitute for C. Marion Dodson. Dodson would later enlist and serve as doctor on a quarantined Union ship in the South. Joshua enlisted with the 3rd Md., Company F with Major Wharton in Baltimore for nine months. In March 1863 he was promoted to Sergeant and in May promoted to 1st Sergeant. He mustered out August 3, 1863 in Baltimore.

Joshua and his wife Josephine lived in St. Michaels after the War, where he made a living as an oysterman. They had several children. Joshua filed for pension in 1890 and died December 2, 1913 in St. Michaels where he is buried with Josephine in Olivet Cemetery.

Ford, Gustavus L. Private

Gustavus L. Ford was born in 1843, the son of Littleton D. Ford of Talbot County, Md. They lived in the St. Michaels area. Gustavus enlisted in the 1st E. Shore September 11, 1861 in St. Michaels with the written consent of his mother. He was 5' 3 ½" tall with a dark complexion, grey eyes and dark hair. He had worked as a sailor until the War. He mustered out August 16, 1862 in Newtown.

Gustavus re-enlisted in Purnells Legion, Cavalry, Company C September 17, 1862 with Theodore Clayton in Baltimore. He was on detached service at Smyrna, Delaware from May to July 1863. On February 14, 1865 he transferred to the 8th Md., Company I. He mustered out May 31, 1865 in Arlington Heights, Va.

Gustavus married Annie E. and filed for pension in 1891. He died about 1902.

Ford, John T. Private

John T. Ford was born 1833 in Talbot County, Md. John "Plum" worked as an oysterman before the War began. He was 5' 7 ½" tall with a dark complexion, blue eyes and brown hair. He enlisted in the 1st E. S. Md. Vols. September 24, 1861 with J. C. Henry in St. Michaels. June 27, 1862 he was absent from his company on detached service at Washington D.C. It appears that his assignment was to assist 1st Lieut. Coburn in taking Private Patrick Henrettie to the insane asylum. John mustered out August 16, 1862 in Newtown.

After the War "Plum" went back to oystering, living with his wife Sarah on East Chestnut St. in St. Michaels. He was murdered and is buried in Olivet Cemetery, St. Luke's United Methodist Church, St. Michaels.

Gannon, James E. Private

James E. Gannon was born in Cecil County, Delaware in 1840 . November 16, 1861 he enlisted in the 1st E. S. with J. C. Henry in Easton. He stood 5' 11" tall with a light complexion, grey eyes and dark hair. Before the war he had been working as an iron molder. He mustered out August 16, 1862 in Newtown.

James re-enlisted September 5, 1862 with Purnells Legion, Cavalry Company C, in Baltimore. May and June 1863 he was on detached service at Smyrna, Delaware. In July and August of the following year, he was absent from his company, being sick in the U. S. General Hospital. November 17, 1864 he transferred to the 8th Md., Company I. He was sick in the City Point, Va. Hospital in the Spring of 1865 and mustered out May 31, 1865 at Arlington Heights, Va.

Geoghegan, Philemon 4th Sergeant

Philemon Geoghegan was born 1834, probably in Dorchester County, Md. He was living in 1850 with James Plasterfield, a ships carpenter, perhaps as an apprentice. Philemon was 5' 7 ½" tall, with grey eyes and brown hair. He appears to have married Margaret E. Cox in 1858. September 11, 1861 he enlisted with the 1st E. S. Md. Vols. in Cambridge. He mustered out August 16, 1862 in Newtown. Shortly thereafter, Philemon was drafted in the Dorchester County Draft. It is uncertain whether he served after being drafted. He died July 15, 1866 in Baltimore and his widow Margaret filed for pension in 1890.

Haddaway, Daniel W. Private

Daniel W. Haddaway was born 1840 to Hugh and Mary A. Haddaway of Talbot County. Daniel enlisted with the 1st E. Shore. October 2, 1861 in St. Michaels. His brother John (below) enlisted the next day. They both mustered out August 16, 1862 in Newtown. After the War, Daniel lived with his wife Ann and their family in the Bay Hundred area of Talbot County, working on the water oystering. They lived in Tilghman in 1890 when he filed for pension. He died February 8, 1921 in Tilghman. His widow Annie filed for pension March 18, 1921.

Haddaway, John S. Private

John S. Haddaway was born 1835 in Talbot County, Md. to Hugh and Mary A. Haddaway. John enlisted with the 1st E. S. the day after his brother Daniel, October 3, 1861 with J. C. Henry in Cambridge. John stood 6' 2" tall and had a dark complexion, grey eyes and light hair. He worked as a sailor. John and Daniel both mustered out August 16, 1862 in Newtown.

After the War John returned to working on the water, oystering in the Bay Hundred area of Talbot County. He and his wife Mary later moved to Oxford. John filed for pension in 1886. His widow filed 1910.

Haddaway, William Henry Private

William Henry Haddaway was the son of William and Susan Seymore Haddaway of Talbot County, Md. He was born October 19, 1843 or 1845. He was 5' 7" tall, with a light complexion, grey eyes and light hair. He worked as a farmer. He enlisted with the 1st E. S. October 2, 1861 in St. Michaels. He appears to have been the youngest in Company A. He mustered out August 16, 1862 in Newtown.

William re-enlisted with the 11th Md., Company A May 27, 1864 with Lieut. William E. Atwell in Baltimore for one hundred days. He mustered out October 1, 1864 in Baltimore. He filed for pension in 1898 and died December 15, 1901.

Harris, William J. Private

William J. Harris was born in 1840 in Delaware. October 3, 1861 William enlisted with the 1st E. S. Md. Vols. with W. Newton in East New Market. He stood 6' tall and had a light complexion, blue eyes and light hair. He had been employed as a blacksmith. He mustered out August 16, 1862 in Newtown. He filed for pension in 1889.

Henrettie, Patrick Private

Patrick Henrettie was born in Baltimore, Md. in 1840. Patrick enlisted in the 1st E. S. Vols. October 2, 1861 in St. Michaels. He was 5' 11 ½" tall, with grey eyes and light hair. He had been working as a sailor until his enlistment. June 29, 1862 he was taken to Washington, D.C. by 1st Lieut. Thomas H. Coburn, Private Wrightson Spedden and Private John T. Ford of Company A where he was admitted to the mental ward in the Government Hospital for the Insane. A letter in his military records dated June 26 written by Capt. Henry from Princess Anne, Md. notes that he had been insane for two months past, had received no medical treatment and had been confined in the county jail for the past ten days. The letter further states that he became insane after enlistment. Patrick was sent to the asylum by order of General Dix. August 16, 1862, Patrick mustered out with the rest of the company. December 29, 1862 it was recommended that Patrick be discharged from the hospital and be delivered to the custody of his family.

Hodson, Joseph H. Private

Joseph H. Hodson was born in "Dorset County" (Dorchester) Md. in 1843. He was likely the son of John H. and Elizabeth Ann Hooper Hodson. His family lived for a time in Dorchester County, 1st Election District and in1860 they moved to Baltimore where Joseph worked as a mariner. September 11, 1861 Joseph enlisted with the 1st E. S. Vols. with J. C. Henry in East New Market. He stood 5' 5" tall and had a light complexion, blue eyes and light hair. He had been making his living as a sailor. He mustered out August 16, 1862 in Drummondtown, Va.

In 1870 Joseph's mother Elizabeth had moved back to Dorchester County, apparently widowed and farming to support herself and three nearly grown children. Joseph is not listed as living with them. He may have died, as his mother filed for pension in 1881.

Holland, Robert B. Private

Robert B. Holland was born in 1830. On August 24, 1854 he married Harriet Ann Mitchell. September 11, 1861 he enlisted with the 1st E. S. Md. in Cambridge. He mustered out August 16, 1862 in Newtown. In 1880 Robert and Harriet moved to Baltimore City where he worked as a laborer to support his family, including his mother Ann. His widow filed for pension in 1890.

Horseman, Jenkins Private

Jenkins Horseman was born 1840 in "Dorset County" (Dorchester) Md. to Jenkins Horseman Sr. and his 2nd wife Sarah Rawley. By 1850 Sarah had been widowed and married again, marrying George Sulivane in 1845. At the start of the War, Jenkins Jr. was living and working as a farm hand at the farm of J. Murphy near Cambridge.

September 11, 1861 Jenkins enlisted in the 1st E. Shore with J. C. Henry in Cambridge. He was

5' 8" tall, with a light complexion, grey eyes and light hair. He mustered out August 16, 1862 in Drummondtown, Va. June 27, 1863 he re-enlisted in the 2nd Md. Cavalry Company B with Lieut. Miller in Baltimore for six months. In the Fall of 1863 he was sick in the U.S. General Hospital in Annapolis, Md. He returned to his company November 17, 1863 and mustered out January 26, 1864 in Baltimore.

Jenkins married Isabel Lewis in 1864. They lived in the Church Creek area and later Parsons Creek area where he supported his family by farming. He filed for pension in 1870.

The 1880 Dorchester County Census notes Jenkins as wounded in the war.

Howard, George E. Private

George E. Howard was born 1830, probably in Somerset County, Md. March 7, 1862 he enlisted with the 1st E. Shore in Princess Anne, Somerset County, Md. Princess Anne was the winter quarters for Company A. George mustered out August 16, 1862 in Newtown.

Johnson, Edward K. Private

Edward K. Johnson was born 1840. He enlisted September 11, 1861 with the 1st E. S. Vols. in East New Market, Md. On December 31, 1861 he was on detached service. On August 16, 1862 he mustered out in Newtown. Two days later Edward re-enlisted with Purnells Legion, Cavalry Company A in Newtown, furnishing his own horse and equipment. His service with Purnell's Legion would have placed him in Gettysburg, Pa. July 1863. September 1864 thru February 1865 he was detached from his company at headquarters in Eastville, Va., working as a clerk. January 1865 he was recommended for a commission in the 2nd U.S. Colored Cavalry. He mustered out July 28, 1865 in Fortress Monroe, Va. Edward died before December 1913 when his widow Louisa M. Johnson filed for pension while living in Massachusetts.

Jones, William Private

William Jones was born 1833. He enlisted with the 1st E. S. Md. Vols. July 25, 1862 at Newtown. He mustered out with the rest of the company the following month at Drummondtown, Va.

Keiser, John L. Private

John L. Keiser was born 1838. He enlisted with the 1st E. S. Md. Vols. October 14, 1861 in Cambridge and mustered out August 16, 1862 in Newtown.

Kirby, Walter M. Private

Walter M. Kirby was born 1836 in "Dorset County" (Dorchester) Md. He was the son of Henson and Sarah Mills Kirby. Walter enlisted with the 1st E. S. Vols. September 19, 1861 with T. H. Coburn in Cambridge. He stood 5' 8" tall, and had a light complexion, grey eyes and light hair. At the time of enlistment he had been working as a sailor. December 1861 he was promoted to Corporal. June 27, 1862 he was absent on detached service at Washington, D.C., possibly assisting to escort Private Patrick Henrettie to the asylum. Walter was in Philadelphia, Pa. in July 1862 and back in Drummondtown, Va. to muster out August 16, 1862.

Lednum, William Dallas Private

William Dallas Lednum was born around 1844 in Queen Anne's County, Md. In 1860 Dallas was living in Cambridge, working as a printer with Levin Straughen, editor. He was 5' 8" tall with a light complexion, blue eyes and light hair. On September 11, 1861 he enlisted with J. C. Henry in the 1st E. S. Vols. in Cambridge, with the written consent of his father. November 1, 1861 Dallas transferred to the Regimental Band of the 1st Eastern Shore Vols. He appears to have been discharged separately from his company.

After the War, Dallas and his wife Annie R. moved to Philadelphia, Pa. where he worked as a machinist. He filed for pension in 1905 and died March 8, 1910 in Philadelphia.

Lewis, Noah F. Private

Noah F. Lewis was from "Dorset County" (Dorchester), Md., born about 1839. Standing 5' 6" tall, Noah had a light complexion, hazel eyes and brown hair. Before the War he had made his living as a farmer. He enlisted with the 1st E. S. September 23, 1861 with J. C. Henry in Cambridge and mustered out August 16, 1862 in Drummondtown, Va. He re-enlisted October 20, 1862 in Federalsburg, Md with Company G of the 1st E. S. Md. Vols. He was likely with the 1st Eastern Shore July 3, 1863 for the defense of Culp's Hill, Gettysburg, Pa. He appears to have transferred to the 11th Md., Company F and then transferred to the 2nd Md., Company F. April 1865 he caught pneumonia on duty at Fort Delaware and was later admitted to the hospital in Baltimore, Md. Noah mustered out June 15, 1865 in Baltimore.

Marshall, Robert S. Private

Robert S. Marshall was born in 1834. It is uncertain, but Robert may have been the son of John and Sarah Spedden Marshall. He enlisted with the 1st E. S. Vols. in Cambridge September 19, 1861. He mustered out August 16, 1862 in Newtown. Shortly thereafter he was drafted in Dorchester County and hired Frans Simmer from Pennsylvania to take his place as a substitute. After the War Robert lived in Cambridge and filed for pension in 1891.

Merrick, Algernon Private

Algernon Merrick was from "Dorset County" (Dorchester) Md., born in the mid-1820's. In 1848 he married Emily Vickers of East New Market, Md. They lived in the First District of Dorchester County, where Algernon supported his family farming. After they moved to Cambridge, Algernon worked as a sawyer, though some resources appear to read "lawyer". At the time of the War, he stood 5' 5 ½" tall and had a light complexion, with dark eyes and reddish brown hair. On October 3, 1861 he enlisted with the 1st E. S. Md. Vols. with J. C. Henry in East New Market. He was on furlough in Cambridge late June 1862, presenting the question of whether or not he was on the schooner off Shelltown in the time leading up to the company's discharge. He mustered out August 16, 1862 in Newtown.

In the Fall of 1862 during the Dorchester County Draft, Algernon enlisted as a substitute for Jonathan W. B. Todd, enlisting with Battalion A, 1st Light Artillery in Baltimore for nine months and was discharged February 3, 1864 at Culpepper Court House, Va. He enlisted again March 9, 1865 in Easton, Md. with the 5th Md., Company E, again as a substitute; this time for Isaac H. Wright, for one year. He mustered out September 1, 1865 in Fredricksburg, Va.

After the War, Algernon and his wife Emily lived in Vienna and later in East New Market, where he worked as a (sawer / lawyer ?) and later farming. He filed for pension in 1886 and died before 1895 when his widow filed for pension.

Merrick, Lewis W. Private

Lewis W. Merrick was born about 1841 in "Dorset" (Dorchester) County, Md. Lewis enlisted with the 1st E. Shore October 3, 1861 with W. P. Newton in East New Market. At the time he stood 5' 5" and had a light complexion, grey eyes and brown hair. He was employed as a miller. He mustered out August 16, 1862 in Drummondtown, Va.

Lewis re-enlisted August 29, 1862 with Purnells Legion, Cavalry Company C with Thomas Clayton in Baltimore. He was absent from his company in October 1863 on detached service at Laurel, Delaware. January and February 1864 he was awaiting sentence of court martial, sentence unknown. That summer he was absent, sick and was attached to the Lincoln U.S.A. General Hospital. February 14, 1865 Lewis transferred to the 8th Md., Company I. He entered Company I as Sergeant, but two months later he was reduced to Private per Regimental Order. He was mustered out May 31, 1865 in Arlington Heights, Va.

Lewis was predeceased by his first wife, name unknown and October 28, 1891 he married Maggie E. Merrick. Lewis filed for pension in 1893 and died February 14, 1930 in Cambridge, MD.

Miller, John H. Private

John H. Miller was born in Germany December 17, 1839. On October 2, 1861 John enlisted with the 1st E. Shore with J. W. Straughn in St. Michaels. He was 5' 8" tall, with a light complexion, hazel eyes and light hair. He had been working as a farmer. He mustered out August 16, 1862 in Newtown. He appears to have re-enlisted with 1st Md., Company A, as listed on his pension. During his service with the 1st Md., he would have been at Gettysburg in July 1863. He filed for pension in 1890. John lived in Talbot County for a time and later in Baltimore, Md where he found work as a laborer. In his later years, he was a resident of the National Soldiers Home in Elizabeth City, Va, Hospital Ward 3.

Moore, John Private

John Moore was from Baltimore City, Md., born 1840. September 24, 1861 he enlisted in the 1st E. Shore with J. C. Henry in St. Michaels. He was 5' 5" tall, with a light complexion, blue eyes and light hair. He was employed as a baker at the time of his enlistment. He mustered out August 16, 1862 in Newtown. During the Talbot County Draft of 1862, a John Moore was drafted, but not there is currently not enough information to determine if he was the same John Moore recently discharged from Company A.

Mowbray, John M. Private

John M. Mowbray (Mobray) was born 1840, the son of John Mowbray, of Dorchester County, Md. At the start of the War, John (Jr.) was living in Cambridge where he worked as an apprentice to shoemaker Joseph Hopkins. On September 11, 1861 John enlisted with the 1st E. S. Md. Vols. in Cambridge. He mustered out August 16, 1862 in Newtown. After the War John worked as a shoemaker in Baltimore County, with his wife Elizabeth.

Mowbray, Orville T. Corporal

aka Oliver / Olion

Orville T. Mowbray (Mobray) was born about 1835 in Cambridge, Md. At the age of 13 Oliver lived in the household of William Littleton, taylor. On April 12, 1860 Orville married Mary E. Marshall. They lived in the household of Lydia Bradley in Cambridge until the War. On September 11, 1861 he enlisted with the 1st E. S. Vols. in Cambridge, with the rank of Corporal. He mustered out August 16, 1862 in Newtown.

Orville (Oliver) was 5' 11 ½" tall, with a fair complexion, grey eyes and dark hair. He worked as a 'tobacconist' before the War. Six weeks after discharge from the 1st E. S. he enlisted with the 8th Md., Company G with Lieut. Chaney in Baltimore. October 1, 1862 he was promoted to 2nd Sergeant and later reduced to Private. May 5, 1864 he was missing in action during the battle at Wilderness, Va. It was later determined that he was killed in action. His widow Mary filed for pension 1865. Orville was the first casualty of the original Company A, one of two.

Newton, Wilber F. Private aka William F.

Wilber F. Newton was from "Dorset" (Dorchester) County, Md, born 1839. In 1850 he lived in with Thomas Helsby, a wheelwright. He enlisted September 11, 1861 in the 1st E. S. Vols. with J. C. Henry in East New Market. Wilber stood 6' tall, with a light complexion, grey eyes and dark hair. He had been working as a wagon maker and mechanic. December 1, 1861 he was on detached service and later promoted to non-commissioned staff, as Sergeant. As such, he was frequently absent from his unit at various camps. Wilber was discharged September 28, 1864, having completed his term of service.

After the War Wilber (William) and his wife Mary F. lived in Vienna and later in East New Market with their children. He supported their family by farming. Wilber died 1892-3. Mary filed for pension in 1893.

North, Charles E. Private

Charles E. North was born 1843. He enlisted September 11, 1861 in the 1st E. S. Md. in Cambridge, Md. He mustered out in Drummondtown, Va. August 16, 1862. After the War Charles and his wife Mollie lived in Baltimore, where he kept a restaurant.

Paul, James H. Private

James H. Paul was born about 1838 in Dorchester County, Md. At the start of the War James was 5' 10" tall, had a ruddy complexion, grey eyes and dark hair and worked as a farm laborer. James enlisted in the 1st E. S. Md. Vols. October 14, 1861 in Cambridge and mustered out August 16, 1862 in Newtown. The following summer James enlisted in the 3rd Md., Company B August 7, 1863 in Baltimore. He mustered out in Vicksburg, Miss. September 7, 1865.

James filed for pension in 1885. He and his wife Mary A. lived in the Williamsburg area of Dorchester County in 1900. James died August 11, 1912 & his widow filed for pension that same year.

Paul, John Private

John Paul was from "Dorset" (Dorchester) County, Md. and was born 1838, the son of Jonathon and Margaret Paul. John married Elizabeth A. Reese October 21, 1857. John and Elizabeth lived near Cambridge where they farmed. John stood 5' 4" and had a dark complexion, hazel eyes and dark hair. John enlisted in the 1st E. S. Vols. with J. C. Henry in Cambridge. In February 1862 he was absent from his company on furlough in Cambridge. A certificate verified by a doctor declared him unable to return to duty. He mustered out August 16, 1862.

Shortly after, on October 15, 1862, John was drafted and reported to Camp Bradford, Md. November 22, 1862. He was enlisted into the 3rd Md. Company F on February 21, 1863 in Baltimore by Major Wharton for nine months. The same day, he was promoted to Corporal. In the spring of 1863 he was sick at

U.S.A. General Hospital, Fairfax Seminary, Va. He mustered out September 2, 1863 in Baltimore.

After the War John and Elizabeth lived in Cambridge, where John worked at the mill. He filed for pension in late 1880.

Paul, Levin Private

Levin Paul was born 1817 in "Dorset" (Dorchester) County, Md. April 6, 1836 Levin married Mary Ann Lord. When the War began, Levin was 5' 5 ½" tall, with a dark complexion, blue eyes and dark hair. He had been making his living as a farmer. On September 16, 1861 he enlisted with the 1st E. S. Vols. with J. C. Henry in Cambridge and mustered out August 16, 1862 in Newtown.

Levin and Mary lived in the Vienna area after the War, where he continued to farm. He died in the 1870's.

Phillips, James R. Private

James R. Phillips was born 1842 in "Dorset" (Dorchester) County, Md. He lived with his family in the Cornersville area where they farmed. He was 5' 11" tall with a dark complexion, grey eyes and dark hair. On September 11, 1861 he enlisted in the 1st E. S. with J. H. Coburn in Cambridge. He mustered out August 16, 1862 in Newtown. After the War James and his wife Sallie lived in the area of Vienna, Md.

Ricketts, John H. Private

John H. Ricketts is somewhat of a mystery. There is no military record for a John H. Ricketts in Company A, 1st Eastern Shore Volunteers. There is however a notation dated February 5, 1904 that suggests that John H. O. Richards of Company A was re-filed as John H. Ricketts. There is also a military record for a John H. Ricketts in Company H, enlisting later in the War. However, John H. Rickett's pension record clearly states that he was in Company A. The supporting papers in the pension file clearly site Company A and make no mention of Company H, nor is there any mention of any re-enlistment. In an affidavit,

John says he came down with typhoid fever shortly after his discharge from Company A and when he was nearly recovered from that, a team of horses ran away with him, breaking his knee cap and making him "no longer fit for service after that." This accident would have prevented him from re-enlisting in Co. H.

John H. Ricketts who joined Company H, enlisted April 8, 1864 in Easton, Md.. His records state that he was 18 years old, born in Sussex County, Delaware. He worked as a sailor, was 5' 8" tall, with a fair complexion, blue eyes and sandy hair. He transferred to 11th Md. Company F on February 23, 1865.

No further information has been found to confirm whether or not John H. Ricketts was in one company or the other. Perhaps there were two men with the same name, though census records do not identify either of them.

Robinson, Josiah F. Private

Josiah (Joseph) F. Robinson was born in "Dorset" (Dorchester) County, Md. in 1831. Josiah was 5' 11 ½" tall with a light complexion, blue eyes and brown hair. He was a shoemaker by trade. He married Annie Eliza Marshall and lived in Cambridge. On September 11, 1861 he enlisted with the 1st E. S. Vols. with J. C. Henry in Cambridge. In October 1861 Josiah was absent from his company on detached service to guard the steamer Balloon on its way to Salisbury, Md. He mustered out August 16, 1862 in Drummondtown, Va.

After the War, Josiah and his family lived in Cambridge where he continued working as shoemaker. He filed for pension in 1895.

Robinson, William T. 1st Sergeant

William T. Robinson was born in Cambridge 1835. In 1858 he married Margaret A. Reed. Before the War, William lived with his family in Cambridge and worked as a printer. He stood 5' 5 ½" tall and had a light complexion, blue eyes and dark hair. He enlisted September 11, 1861 in the 1st E. S. with J. C. Henry in Cambridge. In October 1861 he was promoted from clerk to Colonel. The following month he was transferred to Non-commissioned Staff and promoted to Sergeant Major.

On April 18, 1862 William was promoted from Non-commissioned Staff to 1st Lieutenant in Drummondtown, Va. Spring 1863 he was absent on detached service for two days on the Eastern Shore of Md.. He was likely at Culp's Hill for the 3rd day of the Battle of Gettysburg, Fall of 1863 he returned to Annapolis and the following year was discharged in Baltimore. He filed for pension in 1899.

Ross, Henry R. Corporal

Henry R. Ross was born 1835. Henry enlisted September 19, 1861 with the 1st Eastern Shore Vols. at East New Market. November 1, 1861 he was promoted to Corporal and mustered out in Newtown the following summer on August 16, 1862.

Shehee, John Henry Private

John Henry Shehee was born in "Dorset County" (Dorchester) Md. in 1831. John married Priscilla Hayward in 1850. He enlisted September 17, 1861 with the 1st Eastern Shore Vols. with J. C. Henry in Cambridge. He stood 5' 10" and had a dark complexion, grey eyes and black hair. He supported his family working as a carpenter. During his term of service in the Home Guard, John was on furlough in Cambridge for about a week late June 1862. Upon his return to his unit, he bunked with Levin Adkins at their Princess Anne barracks. John mustered out August 16, 1862 in Newtown.

After the war, John and his family lived in Vienna, near Levin Adkins and worked as a farmer. He filed for pension in 1886.

Shorter, Hayland Private

Hayland Shorter was born in 1840. Just prior to the War Haylon (Halon) worked on James Marshall's farm near Cambridge. On October 28, 1861 he enlisted in the 1st E. S. in

Cambridge. He transferred briefly to Company E with Capt. Stafford and then back to Company A. He mustered out August 16, 1862 in Newtown.

After the War he worked as a laborer and farmer living with family near John Shehee. They lived in the Vienna area and later Hooper's Island. He filed for pension in 1891.

Shorter, John Private

John Shorter was born 1842 in "Dorset" (Dorchester) County, Md., the son of John and Mary (Polly) Paul Shorter. John was raised by his mother and grandmother Miny Paul after his father died. At age 19 he enlisted in the 1st E. Shore October 21, 1861 by Levin Paul in Cambridge. He was 5' 4" tall, with a light complexion, blue eyes and light hair. He had been working as a farmer before the War. He transferred briefly to Company E with Capt. Stafford and transferred back to Company A a short time later. He mustered out August 16, 1862 in Newtown.

Shorter, William T. Private

William T. Shorter was born 1838 in Dorchester County, the son of William and Thimsy Shorter. October 19, 1861 William enlisted with the 1st E. S. Vols. in Cambridge with Levin Paul. He was 5' 7" tall, with a light complexion, blue eyes and light hair. He made his living as a farmer. He mustered out August 16, 1862 in Newtown.

Simms, Robert L. Private

Robert L. Simms was born 1835 in Talbot County, Md., St. Michaels District. He was the son of John and Sarah Simms. He enlisted in the 1st Eastern Shore October 2, 1861 in St. Michaels. After a brief time with Capt. Stafford's Company E, Robert transferred back to Company A and mustered out August 16, 1862 in Newtown. Robert was drafted shortly after in the Talbot Draft and was discharged from reporting for duty.

Robert and his wife Mary A. lived in Talbot County after the War, where he worked as a farm laborer. He filed for pension in 1879 and died before 1882.

Smith, Henry Hooper Private

Henry Hooper Smith was from Dorset (Dorchester) County, Md. He was born 1833 to Henry and Ellenor Smith. On September 11, 1861 Hooper enlisted in the 1st E. S. Vols. with J. C. Henry in Cambridge. He stood 5' 4" tall with a light complexion, grey eyes and light hair. Hooper made a living as a farmer before the War. He was joined in Company A by his younger brother Joseph. They mustered out August 16, 1862 in Newtown.

Within a couple of weeks of his discharge, Hooper re-enlisted in Purnells Legion Cavalry Company C with Theodore Clayton in Baltimore. He was absent, sick in Mt. Pleasant, U.S.A. General Hospital in Washington, D.C. on a couple of occasions. He transferred with the rest of his regiment to the 8th Md., where he joined Company I as Corporal. February 14, 1865 he mustered out at Arlington Heights, Va.

Smith, Joseph Private

Joseph Smith was born 1840 in "Dorset" Dorchester County, Md., the son of Henry and Ellenor Smith. Joseph was 5' 8 ½" tall, with a light complexion, blue eyes and light hair. Before the War he worked as a farmer. Joseph and his brother Hooper enlisted in the 1st E. Shore with J. C. Henry in Cambridge September 11, 1861. They both mustered out August 16, 1862 in Newtown, Md.

Smith, Joseph M. Private

Joseph M. Smith was from Dorchester County, Md., born about 1840, the son of Charles T. and Arietta Smoots Smith. Joseph stood 5' 7" tall with a light complexion, blue eyes and light hair. Before the War he worked as a sailor. He enlisted September 11, 1861 with the 1st E. S. Vols. in Federalsburg with J.

C. Henry. He briefly transferred to Company E with Capt. Stafford and transferred back into Company A in November 1861. Joseph deserted with two fellow soldiers August 1, 1862.

Snow, Thomas W. Private

Thomas W. Snow was born in Talbot County, Md. in 1829. Thomas married Sarah Elizabeth Twilley January 7, 1858. They lived in Cambridge, where Thomas kept a boarding house and worked as a carpenter. On September 11, 1861 Thomas joined the 1st Eastern Shore Vols. with J. C. Henry in Cambridge. He was 5' 11" tall, with a light complexion, blue eyes and brown hair. According to his military record he worked repairing the hospital in October, presumably in Cambridge. He mustered out August 16, 1862 in Newtown.

It appears that Thomas died before 1870, as his wife and son Edgar were living in Baltimore, keeping boarders. Elizabeth remarried and filed for pension as Elizabeth Parker with her son Edgar.

Spedden, Martin L. Private

Martin L. Spedden was the son of William H. and Sarah Marshall Spedden, born in 1841. They lived in Dorchester County, Md. On September 11, 1861 Martin enlisted with the 1st Eastern Shore Md. Infantry in Cambridge. He mustered out in Newtown August 16, 1862. Following the War, Martin married Mary V. Matthews in 1866 and moved to Baltimore where he worked as an engineer. He filed for pension in 1892.

Spedden, Wrightson Corporal

Wrightson Spedden was born 1841 in Dorchester County, Md., the son of Robert Brannock Spedden and Elizabeth Wrightson Spedden. His father died when Wrightson was in his teens and he and his brother Robert moved with their mother to live with Thomas Wrightson, likely their uncle. They lived in Cornersville in Dorchester County where they made their living as farmers. Wrightson was 5' 10" with a light complexion, grey eyes and light hair. He joined the 1st E. S. Md. Vols. September 11, 1861 in Cambridge with J. H. Coburn. June 27, 1862 he was absent from his company on detached service at Washington, D. C. while escorting Private Henrettie to the Asylum for the Insane. He was promoted to Corporal the summer of 1862 and mustered out August 16, 1862 in Newtown.

Wrightson was later drafted and paid Charles Otto of Baltimore to take his place as substitute. Wrightson married Clara H. on January 19, 1870. They lived in the Neck District of Dorchester County, where he supported his large family by farming. He later lived in Hills Point, Dorchester County and filed for pension in 1890.

Stevens, Thomas W. A. Private

Thomas W. A. Stevens was born about 1835. On April 13, 1857 he married Elizabeth R. Thompson in Dorchester County. He was a farmer and stood 5' 9 ½" tall, with a light complexion, blue eyes and brown hair. On September 19, 1861 he enlisted in the 1st Eastern Shore in Cambridge. He mustered out of service August 16, 1862 in Drummondtown, Va..

Thomas was drafted later in the War and enlisted with Purnell's Legion Cavalry Company A. He mustered out May 12, 1865 in Baltimore.

Stewart, Charles E. Private

Charles E. Stewart was from Dorchester County, Md. He was born 1842 to Thomas J. and Ann Maria LeCompte Stewart. He was 5' 7" tall, with a light complexion, hazel eyes and light hair. He worked as a farmer. His father died in the early 1850's; his mother married Levin Wheeler in 1855. January 1, 1862 Charles joined the 1st Eastern Shore Md. Vols. with J. C. Henry in Cambridge. He mustered out in Drummondtown, Va. August 16, 1862. In the 1870 Dorchester County Census, Charles is listed as a disabled soldier living in Cambridge with his mother, apparently widowed as Levin is not listed in the household. Since Company A did not participate in any battle, the nature of Charles' disability is unknown. He was still living with his mother in Cambridge in 1880.

Straughn, James W. Sergeant

James W. Straughn was born 1837 to James and Eliza Ann Willis Straughn. His family lived in Cambridge, Md. where his father was a merchant. September 11, 1861 James enlisted with the 1st Eastern Shore Volunteers in Cambridge and was promoted to Sergeant. That winter he was promoted to 2nd Sergeant. He was mustered out August 16, 1862 in Drummondtown, Va..

Sweed, William B. Private

William B. Sweed was born 1842. He joined the 1st Eastern Shore Md. Volunteers September 11, 1861 in East New Market, Md.. He died in winter quarters in Princess Anne, Md. of pneumonia March 28, 1862. Private Sweed was the first casualty of Company A and the only casualty in the Company to occur during their year of service.

Sylvester, Isaac H. Private

Isaac H. Sylvester was born in Caroline County, Md. in 1839. On October 28, 1861 Isaac joined the 1st E. Shore with J. C. Henry in the St. Michaels/Royal Oak area. He was 5' 7" tall, with a light complexion, blue eyes and light hair. Until the War he had been working as a farmer. He mustered out August 16, 1862 in Newtown.

Isaac re-enlisted in Purnell's Legion Cavalry Company A on September 1, 1862 in Newtown. He was absent from this company without leave, having deserted November 10, 1862. He was apprehended the following spring and court martialed. Isaac's widow Fannie moved to Delaware and filed for pension in 1892.

Tarr, William H. Corporal

William H. Tarr was born in 1839 to John and Lydia Tarr of St. Michaels, Md.. William enlisted in the 1st E. S. Md. Vols. September 11, 1861 in St. Michaels. He stood 5' 6", with hazel eyes and black hair and had been working as a waterman before his enlistment. He mustered out in Newtown, Md. August 16, 1862.

Months later, William was paid by Samuel T. Harris as a substitute and he re-enlisted with the 4th Md. Company D. At the time of his enlistment, William had a tattoo, described as four small dots in Indian ink on his left hand. He enlisted February 13, 1863 with Captain Orem in Baltimore, agreeing to serve for nine months. He was received into service at Camp Hicks, Easton, Md. which was used as a rendezvous camp for the Eastern Shore during the draft of 1862. William served with Captain A. C. Williams and was promoted to Corporal following his enlistment.

After the War William returned to his family in St. Michaels where he made his living as an oysterman. He filed for pension in 1890 and again in 1908. He died April 4, 1920 at Love Point, Kent Island, Md..

Thomas, Charles H. Private

Charles H. Thomas was born 1838, the son of Samuel and Sarah A. Soward Thomas. Charles lived in the Cornersville area of Dorchester County, Md. where he worked as a farm hand with his father. September 11, 1861 Charles enlisted in the 1st E. S. Vols. in Cambridge. He mustered out August 16, 1862 in Newtown, Md..

Todd, William M. Private

William M. Todd was born about 1842. On September 11, 1861 William enlisted with the 1st Eastern Shore in Cambridge, with the written consent of his father. He mustered out August 16, 1862 in Newtown, Md.. William re-enlisted September 30, 1862 in Baltimore, Md. with the 8th Maryland

Company G, . He was wounded in action at Laurel Hill, Va. May 11, 1864 and admitted to the Judiciary Square General Hospital in Washington, D.C. with a gun shot to the left leg. He returned to duty August 12, 1864 and mustered out May 31, 1865. He filed for pension in 1891.

Townsend, William J. Private

William J. Townsend was born about 1840. On October 12, 1861 William joined the 1st Eastern Shore Infantry at Cambridge, Md.. He briefly transferred to Captain Stafford's Company E and in November transferred back to Company A with Captain Henry. He mustered out August 16, 1862 in Newtown, Md..

William married Rachel F. Carroll September 20, 1862. They lived in Vienna after the War where he supported his family as a laborer. He died before 1886, when Rachel filed for pension.

Tucker, Thomas T. Private

Thomas T. Tucker was born about 1840. He enlisted in the 1st Eastern Shore on October 3, 1861 in East New Market, Md. and mustered out September 18, 1862 in Newtown, Md.. As the War neared its end, Thomas married Frances Arnett March 8, 1865 in Dorchester County. After the War they lived in Cambridge where Thomas worked as a farmer. They later moved to East New Market. Thomas died August 8, 1914 in Springfield (?). His widow filed for pension that same year.

Warren, Joseph W. Private

Joseph W. Warren was born about 1842. He enlisted with the 1st E. Shore Vols. September 11, 1861 in Cambridge and mustered out August 16, 1862 in Drummondtown, Va..

Way, Charles H. Private

Charles H. Way was born in New York City, NY. in 1839. He enlisted with the 1st Eastern Shore October 22, 1861 with J. C. Henry in St. Michaels. He was 5' 4" tall, with a dark complexion, hazel eyes and dark hair. Before his enlistment he had been employed as a sailor. Charles transferred to Company E with Captain George W. Evans and after a short time, transferred back to Company A. He mustered out August 16, 1862 in Drummondtown, Va..

Charles was drafted within months of his discharge and he re-enlisted with, the 11th Maryland Company A for one hundred days. He mustered out September 15, 1864 in Mourovia B&O Railroad where he re-enlisted three days later with Company B of the same regiment.

After the War Charles worked as a farmer in the St. Michaels area, living in the household of Thomas Wayman. He filed for pension in 1885. He died about 1886.

West, George W. Private

George W. West was born about 1840 in St. Michaels, Md.. George was raised by his grandparents, Garrettson & Elizabeth Gossage West in St. Michaels. At the start of the War, he was working as an oysterman and living with his grandmother Elizabeth Gossage West and his Aunt Hester West Harrison's family. George stood 5' 11" tall and had a dark complexion, blue eyes and brown hair. He joined the 1st E. Shore Vols. September 24, 1861 with J. C. Henry in St. Michaels. He was absent from his company in October 1861 on detached service to guard the steamer Balloon when it was sent to Salisbury, Md.. He mustered out August 16, 1862 in Newtown, Md.

The draft in Talbot County was held the Fall of 1862 and George went back into service as a substitute for Jonathan T. Harrison, Jr. He enlisted with the 3rd Md. Company D, and mustered out July 31, 1865 at Delaney House, Washington, D.C. He filed for pension in 1890. Though the date of his death is not known, George is buried in Olivet Cemetery, St. Michaels, Md. His grave is marked with a Civil War marker for his service in the 3rd Md. Infantry.

Wherrett, Thomas H. Sergeant

Thomas H. Wherrett was from Talbot County, Md., born 1838 the son of William and Rebecca Lucas Wherrett. The family moved to Cambridge where his father worked as a cabinet maker, apparently after the death of Thomas' mother. Thomas enlisted with the 1st Eastern Shore September 11, 1861 with J. C. Henry in Cambridge. He was 5' 6" tall, with light complexion, grey eyes and light hair. Before his enlistment, he had been employed as a tailor. He mustered out August 16, 1862 in Drummondtown, Va..

Thomas re-enlisted with the 8th Md. Company G on September 30, 1862 in Baltimore, Md. with Lieut. Chaney. January 1863 he was promoted to 3rd Corporal and in May of the same year he was promoted to 1st Corporal. He was wounded in the stomach at Spottsylvania Court House, Va. May 8, 1864 and was captured. He was admitted to the hospital in Richmond, was later paroled at Aikus Landing, Va. and reported to Camp Parole, Annapolis, Md. on August 19, 1864. Thomas was promoted again September 1, 1864, to Sergeant. That Fall, his father wrote General Wallace to request a furlough. A furlough was finally granted, and he returned home to Cambridge until November 19, 1864. However, Thomas delayed returning to duty and was arrested in Baltimore in early December. He was confined as a result and returned to duty in the Spring of 1865, without trial.

Thomas filed for pension in 1890 in Cambridge and died before1907 when Mary L. Wherrett filed for pension as his widow.

Winterbottom, Harrison T. Orderly Sergeant

Harrison T. Winterbottom was from Cambridge, Md., born the son of Harrison and Rachel Abbett Winterbottom in 1828. From the census records it appears that by 1850 both parents were deceased and Harrison Jr. was living with his brother Henry and their widowed sister Ann M. Winterbottom Todd with her two young children. Harrison supported the family as a boot and shoemaker in Cambridge.

At the start of the War, he left a wife and two children to join the 1st E. S. Md Vols. He was 5' 8 ½" tall, with light complexion, blue eyes and light hair. He enlisted September 11, 1861 with J. C. Henry in Cambridge. On November 1, 1861 he was promoted to 1st Sergeant. He was on leave in Cambridge in early August 1862 and was returning to duty with Sgt. Bothum and Sgt. Dail as the events began leading to the discharge of Company A. He mustered out with the rest of the company August 16, 1862 in Newtown, Md..

After the War Harrison returned to Mary and the children in Cambridge, continuing his trade as a shoemaker. He is listed in the census records adjacent to Col. James Wallace, who had returned to his profession as a lawyer. Later Harrison's occupation is found listed as magistrate. In 1903 his widow, Mary E. Winterbottom filed for pension.

Woodrow, William E. Corporal

William E. Woodrow was born in 1840 in Cecil County, Md.. By 1860 he had moved to Cornersville, Dorchester County and was a carpenter's apprentice living in the household of Henry Cook. William stood 5' 10" tall and had a light complexion, hazel eyes and brown hair. He enlisted with the 1st E. Shore Vols. September 19, 1861 with T. H. Coburn in Cambridge and mustered out August 16, 1862 in Newtown, Md..

That same Fall, William was drafted back into service and he enlisted with the 3rd Maryland Company F in Baltimore, Md.. Commissioned for nine months, he resigned after only a month "believing myself incompetent to occupy my present position". He mustered out in September 1863 in Baltimore.

After the War William returned to his trade as a carpenter in Cornersville. From the census records it appears that he married twice, the second time to Sarah. William filed for pension in 1898 and again in 1902.

i After the war, Sgt. Levin Bothum married Ann Kirby, daughter of Major Kirby, commander of Camp Kirby in Easton, Md. His notes were written some years after the war, in the back pages of the Camp Kirby ledger. The Camp Kirby Ledger is the property of the Dorchester County Historical Society.

ii Peter Kolchin, American Slavery: 1619-1877, New York: Hill and Wang, 1993, pp.81-82 http://en.wikipedia.org/wiki/Maryland#cite_note-44

iii James Ford Rhodes, History of the Civil War, 1861-1865, The Macmillan Company, New York, 1917, p.19. http://en.wikipedia.org/wiki/Baltimore_riot_of_1861#cite_note-7

iv J.M. Stoddart, Stoddart's Encyclopaedia Americana: A Dictionary of Arts, Sciences, & General Literature (1884) pg.351 http://books.google.com/books?id=fl1MAAAAMAAJ&pg=PA351#v=onepage&q&f=false

v John E. Rastall papers, University of Maryland, Digital Archive, Collection No, 98-146 http://hdl.handle.net/1903.1/1327 NOTE: Elijah Parish Lovejoy was an active abolitionist many years before the Civil War broke out.

vi John C. Henry letter, Dorchester County Historical Society, Genealogy Collection. NOTE: Flag of Truce letter was any letter intended to be sent across enemy lines and was marked "Flag of Truce" on the outer envelope. Names were often left out, or indicated by initials only to prevent identification. Such letters were often addressed & signed to further prevent identification, hence the letter to his mother was address as to a friend & signed with J. C.'s middle initial.

vii J. Thomas Scharf, History of Western Maryland, Genealogical Publishing Company, (2003) p.318.

viii Bothum's Account (see i.) Potter's Landing was first established in the mid 1700's by Zabdiel Potter, a sea captain from Rhode Island and became a key early port for shipping tobacco and other products to Baltimore. When Capt. Potter was lost at sea, his sons continued the shipping trade. In 1847 the Potter family sold the property of Potter's Hall to Col. John Arthur Willis who changed the name to Williston.

ix Letter to Editor of local newspaper by John E. Rastall from the Wisconsin Veterans' Home Sept. 8, 1924. Copy from Dorchester County Historical Society collection.

x Levin Bothum's account (see i.).

xi Darrell N. Middleton, The Second Regiment Delaware Volunteers, Georgetown, DE (2005) Henry Hayes Lockwood was born in Kent County, Delaware August 17, 1814. He had served in the Seminole Wars and a professor of mathematics at the U. S. Naval Academy at the start of the War. He was considered an expert in infantry tactics. He was commissioned Brigadier General August 8, 1861. After the war he returned to his teaching position at the Naval Academy and retired from service August 18, 1876. He died December 7, 1899 and is buried with his wife and son at the Naval Academy in Annapolis, Md. He is the only Army General buried on the grounds of a Naval facility.

xii Interesting Sketch of the Eastern Shore Regiment, Letter to Newspaper, by John E. Rastall (see ix.)

xiii Letter to Editor, unnamed soldier of the 1st Eastern Shore Home Guard to the Cambridge Herald, Dorchester County Public Library, microfilm.

xiv Drummondtown, Va. was established in 1787. The town was renamed Accomac in 1893. According to The Origin of Certain Place Names in the United States by Henry Gannett (1905) pg.16, the word Accomac (also spelled Accomack) is from an Native American word meaning 'on the other side'. http://books.google.com/books?id=BqwPAAAAIAAJ&pg=PA16#vonepage&q&f=false

xv Alton Brooks Parker Barnes, Pungoteague to Petersburg, Vol. II, Eastern Shore Soldiers, The Civil War 1858 – 1865

xvi Fortress Monroe is located in Hampton, mainland Virginia. The six-sided stone fort is surrounded by a moat and was built in 1834 on the site of an early colonial fort. In spite of its location in Confederate Virginia, Fortress Monroe remained in Union hands throughout the war.

xvii Newtown, Md., originally called Stevens Landing (or Stevens Ferry) was established in the late 1600's on the south side of the Pocomoke River. Newtown (or New Town) was incorporated in 1865, and reincorporated as Pocomoke in 1878. According to The Origin of Certain Place Names in the United States by Henry Gannett (1905) pg.248, the word 'pocomoke' comes from the Native American word for 'broken by knolls'. http://books.google.com/books?id=BqwPAAAAIAAJ&pg=PA248#vonepage&q&f=false

xviii Kirk Mariner, True Tales of the Eastern Shore, Miona Publications.

xix 'Secesh': A slang term referring to a Secessionist, a supporter of the Confederate cause.

xx Mariner, (see xix.)

xxi Rastall Collection (see v.)

xxii Bell Irvin Wiley, (The) Life of Johnny Reb, The Common Soldier of the Confederacy, Louisiana State University Press

xxiii Rastall Collection (see v.) John E. Rastall was born July 23, 1840 in Cheltenham, Gloucestershire, England. His family immigrated to Milwaukee,

Wisconsin in 1852-3 where John learned the printing trade, working for the Milwaukee Sentinel and Beloit Herald. He joined a group of abolitionists from Wisconsin in the Free State Army in Kansas and at the start of the Civil War, joined the 5th Wisconsin Infantry, U.S. Shortly thereafter he was discharged and accepted a commission as 1st Lieut. Adjutant of the 1st Eastern Shore. After the war Jack returned to farming and printing in Milwaukee. He moved with his wife and children to Kansas and later to Washington, D.C. where he worked for the U.S. Government Printing Office and retired in the 1910's. Jack died in 1927.

xxiv Jefferson Davis, was born June 3, 1808 in Kentucky. Davis graduated from West Point and fought in the Mexican-American War. In 1861 Davis was chosen as President of the Confederate States of America. He was captured May 10, 1865 and charged with treason. He died December 6, 1889.

xxv Rastall Collection (see v.)

xxvi James Ewell Brown (J.E.B.) Stuart (February 6, 1833 – May 12. 1864) J.E.B. Stuart was commander of the Confederate Cavalry and acted at the 'eyes and ears' of Robert E. Lee's army by gathering information of the the enemy position and surrounding area. Stuart was a graduate of West Point and served in Texas and Kansas with the U.S. Army before resigning when Virginia seceded from the Union. He was fatally wounded at the Battle of Yellow Tavern, near Richmond, Va.

xxvii Robert Edward Lee (January 19, 1807 – October 12, 1870) Robert E. Lee was a career military officer. He was considered an exceptional officer and served in the U.S. Army thirty two years before resigning to join the Confederate Army as commanding general. Lee died of pneumonia after suffering a stroke.

xxviii Napoleon Bonaparte Knight was from Dover, Delaware. He was a student of languages, medicine and law. Knight enlisted briefly with a Confederate regiment, but deserted and returned to Delaware. When George P. Fisher, organizing the 1st Delaware Cavalry, was unable to raise a full regiment, he resigned and appointed his protege N. B. Knight as Major of the new regiment.

xxix Military Records of Company A, 1st Eastern Shore, U.S., www.fold3.com

xxx Watt Island is located nearly mid-way along the Bay side of Eastern Virginia between Chesconessex Creek and Tangier Island. At one time it was inhabited, though much of the island has been washed away by tides and storms. During the Civil War the island was the home of Josiah Parker and it remained in his family until 1908. Today the island has been reduced to a very few acres and is used as an educational tool by the Chesapeake Bay Foundation.

xxxi Bothum's Account (see i.)

xxxii http://www.northamericanforts.com/East/md.html#halleck

xxxiii Bothum's Account (see I)

xxxiv The designation 'without honor' is not to be confused with "dishonorable". A 'dishonorable discharge' is usually the result of a court-martial as a punishment for wrong-doing. The men of Company A were never court-martialed.

xxxv Letter to Commissioner Evans, Washington, D.C. Dated June 27, 1900; pension file of George W. Elliott National Archives, Washington, D.C.

xxxvi Letter to Commissioner Evans, Washington D.C. Dated July 3, 1900; pension file of Thomas H. Coburn National Archives, Washington, D.C.

xxxvii Letter to Commissioner Evans, Washington, D.C. Dated June 27, 1900; pension file of George W. Elliott National Archives, Washington, D.C.

xxxviii General Affidavit of John H. Ricketts 7/9/1900; pension file of John H. Ricketts National Archives, Washington, D.C.

xxxix Letter to H. Clay Evans, Pension Commissioner dated July 3, 1900; Pension file of Thomas H. Coburn. National Archives, Washington, D.C.

xl Pension Appeal (Ricketts & Miller) by Lloyd, AIF National Archives, Washington, D.C.

xli Pension Record of George W. Elliott, National Archives, Washington, D.C.

xlii Pension Record of John H. Miller, National Archives, Washington, D.C.

xliii Shelltown is located in Brinkleys District, Somerset County, Maryland on the north side of the Pocomoke River. In the summer of 1862 the area was occupied by the Whittington family. John P. Whittington was a farmer and lived at Shelltown with his wife Sally and their son Alfred, daughter-in-law Rosina Donoho Whittington and grandchildren. Alfred was a teacher, suggesting there may have been enough families in the area to need a teacher. Isaac Melborn, a merchant from Germany, and a blacksmith named Samuel D. (Melborn, or Whittington) also lived in the household. John and Sally's son John A. Francis Whittington, a ship's carpenter, lived nearby with his wife Susan Ella Beauchamp Whittington and their two sons, as well as Thomas B. Beauchamp and William Adams. With the variety of trades practiced at the site, it would seem to have been more than just a back-country farm. As the 1877 Atlas shows an oyster house, store house and steamboat landing, one might suppose that those businesses had already begun at the time of the Civil War.

xliv Military records. National Archives, Washington, D.C.; www.fold3.com

xlv Rastall Collection (see v.) In another letter, Rastall mentions that Company B was later arrested and placed in custody at Salisbury. There being no brig in which to hold them, they were forced to build their own of logs. Anyone not willing to work would be given bread and water only. When their fort was complete, they were given the chance to redeem themselves. After swearing an oath, *"They were released and a finer company is not in the Regt."*

xlvi Letter of J.C. Henry's daughter Willie. Dorchester County Historical Society Genealogical Collection.

xlvii Official Records of the War of the Rebellion

xlviii From the Pension Record of John H. Ricketts, National Archives, Washington, D.C.

www.ingramcontent.com/pod-product-compliance
Ingram Content Group UK Ltd.
Pitfield, Milton Keynes, MK11 3LW, UK
UKHW041937190726
13854UKWH00004B/1645

9 781105 776762